Theater

VOLUME 47, NUMBER 1

T0341586

Tom Sellar, *Editor*

YALE SCHOOL OF DRAMA
YALE REPERTORY THEATRE

EDITOR   Tom Sellar

GUEST COEDITOR *Show Me the World*   Sigrid Gareis

ASSOCIATE EDITOR   David Bruin

MANAGING EDITORS   Charles O'Malley and Ariel Sibert

STAFF   Michael Breslin, Molly FitzMaurice, Amauta Martson-Firmino, Sophie Siegel-Warren, and Patrick Young

ADVISORY BOARD   James Bundy, Victoria Nolan, Catherine Sheehy

CONTRIBUTING EDITORS   Una Chaudhuri, Liz Diamond, Miriam Felton-Dansky, Elinor Fuchs, Jacob Gallagher-Ross, Gitta Honegger, Shannon Jackson, Jonathan Kalb, Renate Klett, Jennifer Krasinski, James Leverett, Mark Lord, Charles McNulty, Ken Reynolds, Joseph Roach, Marc Robinson, Gordon Rogoff, Daniel Sack, Alisa Solomon, Andrea Tompa, Paul Walsh

AFFILIATED ARTISTS   Marc Bamuthi Joseph, Annie Dorsen, Branden Jacobs-Jenkins, Morgan Jenness, Melanie Joseph, Aaron Landsman, David Levine

Theater is published three times a year (February, May, and November) by Duke University Press, 905 W. Main St., Suite 18B, Durham, NC 27701, on behalf of the Yale School of Drama/Yale Repertory Theatre. For a list of the sources in which *Theater* is indexed and abstracted, see www.dukepress.edu /theater.

SUBMISSIONS AND
EDITORIAL CORRESPONDENCE
See the Duke University Press *Theater* website for detailed submission guidelines: theater.dukejournals.org. Send manuscripts for submission and letters concerning editorial matters to *Theater*, PO BOX 208244, New Haven, CT 06520-8244; theater.magazine @yale.edu.

PERMISSIONS
Photocopies for course or research use that are supplied to the end user at no cost may be made without explicit permission or fee. Photocopies that are provided to the end user for a fee may not be made without payment of permission fees to Duke University Press. Address requests for permission to republish copyrighted material to Rights and Permissions Manager, permissions @dukeupress.edu.

WORLD WIDE WEB
Visit the journal's website at www.theatermagazine.org and Duke University Press Journals at www.dukeupress.edu/journals.

SUBSCRIPTIONS
Direct all orders to Duke University Press, Journals Customer Relations, 905 W. Main St., Suite 18B, Durham, NC 27701. Annual subscription rates: print-plus-electronic institutions, $217; print-only institutions, $206; e-only institutions, $166; e-only individuals, $15; individuals, $30; students, $20. For information on subscriptions to the e-Duke Journals Scholarly Collections, contact libraryrelations@dukeupress.edu. Print subscriptions: add $11 postage and applicable HST (including 5% GST) for Canada; add $14 postage outside the US and Canada. Back volumes (institutions): $206. Single issues: institutions, $69; individuals, $12. For more information, contact Duke University Press Journals at 888-651-0122 (toll-free in the US and Canada) or at 919-688-5134; subscriptions @dukeupress.edu.

ADVERTISEMENTS
Direct inquiries about advertising to Journals Advertising Coordinator, journals_advertising@dukeupress.edu.

DISTRIBUTION
Theater is distributed by Ubiquity Distributors, 607 DeGraw St., Brooklyn, NY 11217; phone: 718-875-5491; fax: 718-875-8047.

© 2017 by Yale School of Drama/ Yale Repertory Theatre
ISSN 0161-0775

Contributors

TILMANN BROSZAT is the artistic and managing director of the biannual SPIELART Festival in Munich, which he founded in 1995. He also is the managing director and producer of the Munich Biennale Festival for Contemporary Music Theatre (since 1988) and the coordinator of Munich's DANCE festival (since 1998).

BORIS CHARMATZ is a dancer and choreographer, and the creator of Musée de la Danse.

KENNETH COLLINS is the writer, director, and visual artist behind Temporary Distortion, a group exploring the tensions and overlaps found among practices in visual art, theater, cinema, and music by working across disciplines to create installations, films, albums, and works for the stage.

THOMAS F. DEFRANTZ is professor and chair of African and African American studies at Duke University and director of SLIPPAGE: Performance, Culture, Technology, a research group that explores emerging technology in live performance applications.

SIGRID GAREIS has cofounded festivals in Moscow, Munich, Nuremberg, and Greifswald. From 2000 to 2009 she was the founding director of Tanzquartier Wien, and from 2011 to 2014 she was the founding general manager of the Academy of the Arts of the World, Cologne. She curates internationally and teaches performance curation at various universities.

JONATHAN KALB has been pondering the marvels and mysteries of German theater since he lived in West Berlin in the 1980s. He is professor of theater at Hunter College, works as resident dramaturg at Theatre for a New Audience, and is currently translating Wedekind's *Lulu* for a new American production.

MICHAEL J. KRAMER teaches history, American studies, and civic engagement at Northwestern University. He serves as dramaturg/historian-in-residence for The Seldoms, a contemporary dance theater company based in Chicago. He is also on the advisory board for Dancing on the Third Coast: The Chicago Dance History Project. Kramer has written for numerous publications. He blogs about art, culture, history, politics, and more at *Culture Rover* (culturerover.net).

ANDRÉ LEPECKI is associate professor in performance studies at New York University. He is an independent curator working on dance and performance and the author of *Singularities: Dance in the Age of Performance* (2016) and *Exhausting Dance: Performance and the Politics of Movement* (2006).

SODJA LOTKER was artistic director of the Prague Quadrennial from 2008 to 2015, and in 2016, the Prague Quadrennial won the 2015–16 EFFE Award for Excellence. She works as a dramaturg for devised theater and has collaborated with, and commissioned work from, Wojtek Zimilski, Lotte van den Berg, Arpad Schilling, Claudia Bosse, and Socìetas Raffaelo Sanzio. She has given lectures at Trinity College, Columbia University, and the Royal Central School of Speech and Drama, and since 2016 she has been the Course Leader of Directing Devised and Object Theatre at DAMU, Prague.

FLORIAN MALZACHER is a critic, dramaturg, and curator and the artistic director of the Impulse Theater Festival in Düsseldorf, Cologne, and Mülheim. From 2006 to 2012 he was coprogrammer of the multidisciplinary arts festival Steirischer Herbst in Graz.

JAY PATHER is associate professor at the University of Cape Town, where he directs the Institute for Creative Arts. He currently curates Infecting the City (Cape Town), the Live Art Festival (Cape Town), and Afrovibes (Amsterdam). Recent publications include articles in *Changing Metropolis II*, *Rogue Urbanism*, and *Performing Cities*.

SUELY ROLNIK is a psychoanalyst and professor at Pontifical Catholic University of São Paulo. Her research focuses on the politics of subjectivization from a transdisciplinary theoretical approach, inseparable from a therapeutic-political pragmatic. Among her books are *Archive Mania* (2011) and, with Félix Guattari, *Molecular Revolution in Brazil* (2007).

TOM SELLAR is editor of *Theater* and professor of dramaturgy and dramatic criticism at Yale School of Drama.

MIRANDA WRIGHT is the founder and executive director of Los Angeles Performance Practice (www.losangeles performancepractice.org) and lead curator for the annual Live Arts Exchange / LAX Festival (www.liveartsexchange.org). She is currently the curatorial artist-in-residence at the Center for the Art of Performance at UCLA, and the artistic program coordinator for the Richard E. Sherwood Award, presented annually by Center Theatre Group to an emerging artist of promise in Los Angeles.

Contents

Title Page:
Section of Countries
and Regions: Serbia,
Prague Quadrennial,
Prague, 2015. Photo:
Martina Novozamska

Inside Back Cover:
LAX Launch Pad,
Bootleg Theater,
Los Angeles, 2013.
Photo:
Amanda Jane Shank

Special thanks are due to our partners in the
"Show Me the World" section: Tilmann Broszat,
director of SPIELART Festival, and Sigrid Gareis, the
conference codirector and this section's guest coeditor,
as well as to Wenzel Bilger from Goethe-Institut
New York. "Show Me the World" was a project of the
SPEILART Festival and the Goethe Institutes in Bogotá,
Cairo, Lagos, Munich, New York, São Paulo, and
Singapore, as well as the NRW KULTURsekretariat,
the Impulse Theater Festival, Theaterwissenschaft
München, the Rignlokschuppen Ruhr, and
the Kulturreferat der Landschauptstadt München.

Up Front

CURATING CRISIS

Tom Sellar

This is the second of two issues *Theater* is devoting to the curation of performance, a highly contested field whose current redefinition holds major implications for theater, dance, and other live forms. Our first issue (*Theater* 44, no. 2, 2014) explored the historical precedents for institutional and independent curators specializing in these forms and looked at why the new nomenclature matters at a moment when forms have converged and why the limitations of producing and presenting structures have become apparent.

This issue of *Theater* continues that conversation with an additional set of interviews with practitioners—such as Boris Charmatz, who redesignated his national dance center in France a "dancing museum"—whose initiatives have opened up new possibilities in the cultural arena. But it also attempts to open the discussion to broader contexts and more socially applied curation: for instance, Thomas F. DeFrantz, in his opening essay, calls for a cultivation of community and a recentering around minoritarian forms, a shift that would embody a new ethics and reflect new American demographic and cultural realities.

In the special section, "Show Me the World," we present three essays adapted and expanded from the 2015 Munich convening of the same name. Held at the Haus der Kunst and under the auspices of the biannual SPIELART Festival, the convening sought to address questions about transnationalism in curating. With enviable resources and infrastructures, European cultural institutions dominate the globe's artistic sector— along with their curators and their preferences and political priorities. How can curation of performance be reimagined to reflect a postcolonial present and future? The essays in this section use theory to stake out new, perhaps more fertile ground for performance, looking to South Africa, Brazil, and elsewhere for an uncolonized and reawakened political imagination. Initiatives such as Shared Spaces—a network of artists, curators, and other professionals founded in 2013, convened in Kinshasa, Ramallah, Zurich, and Durban—have attempted to bridge continental divides. "Show Me the World" looks more analytically at the discourses embedded in curatorial perspectives. The initiative's transnational emphasis suggests something hopeful: an expanded context and widened inquiry for live performance as it makes its way out of theaters and galleries. To address the social, economic, and environmental crises besetting the world today, which know no borders, curators will need to reimagine their practices accordingly.

Students stand on top of the base that once held the statue of Cecil John Rhodes, Cape Town, 2015. Photo: Roger Sedres /Alamy

Theater 47:1 DOI 10.1215/01610775-3710489

I

Bruce Nauman's
Green Light Corridor (1970),
in *Move: Choreographing You*,
the Hayward Gallery, London,
2010. Photo: Alastair Muir

Thomas F. DeFrantz

Identifying the Endgame

What's an Audience or a Public?

To think carefully about the possibilities of curatorial practice in relation to the emergence of audiences and publics, we surely come back to questions of demographics, social relations, and cultural assumptions. In the context of the United States, the proliferation of new performance forms in the 1960s and the establishment of national institutions to administer them in the 1980s led us to discuss these sorts of markers as identity politics and to speak of multicultural programming. We tended to assume the presence of a white masculine audience, artist, and object that would be circulated in the name of art; our progressive politics told us that those majority stakeholders could possibly be augmented by small numbers of audiences of color in relation to a black artist or a white woman artist. These incursions would somehow demonstrate a brief diversity of creative exercise. This sort of programming lasted all the way to the new millennium—did it ever stop?—in performance seasons with one black artist or with visual artist lineups that included a white women's moment among the men. At times, queer white men might be identified as gay, allowing them presence as alternative artists/publics, and also allowing the overexposure that men always have in the world.

Obviously, this approach to curating as though the audience or public were mostly white, peppered with a little bit of color at times, failed. But we went along with the logic for a very long time. If the art, artist, and its venue were conceived to be "straight white masculinist," all the rest of us responded to that core as we imagined ourselves to be potential artists and publics. We tried to see ourselves among the white work, and at times we created counterpublics and dissenting performances. We demanded a Studio Museum in Harlem as a venue to show experimental black work and performance; we supported a Museum of the African Diaspora to demonstrate affinities of black creativity across geography and time. Artists tried to make black work, concerned with black lives, but it was inevitably positioned in "alternative" venues and subject to critiques of

Theater 47:1 DOI 10.1215/01610775-3710429

The Studio Museum
of Harlem with
David Hammons's
*African-American
Flag* (1990),
New York, 2016.
Photo: Jen Davis

The Studio Museum of Harlem with David Hammons's *African-American Flag* (1990), New York, 2016. Photo: Jen Davis

diminished sophistication. Identifying work in terms of a social politics meant that the work could be disparaged or disregarded when its markers of identity became unfashionable. Fantasies of art that might exist outside of race were countered by a reality of being always already in relation to the long-established white norm for art.

In these decades, social relations and cultural assumptions diverted attention away from communities of color as capable of their own ontological production of creative thought and practice. This varied from the black arts movement and its insistence on creativity for audiences of color as something of a right of citizenry. Theater companies, dance companies, and venues for spoken word and visual arts emerged in this era, galvanizing possibilities for communities of color in provocative, sensual, and spiritual performance creativity. These institutions emerged with limited government funding, mostly created by political structures that assumed "colored" versions of white practices of art making, gathering around art, and the becoming-an-artist of those committed to social justice as it was conceived at that time.

After the civil rights era, if there were to be black venues that demonstrated black participation in American cultural life, they would be led by African American administrators who participated in the (larger, white) art scene as best they could. This sort of logic led to some identity-laden venues and circulations of creative expression. Black-led theaters and dance companies, which had always been around in the United States, established themselves as best they could, some with brick and mortar, such as the New Jersey–based Crossroads Theatre Company or the Joan Weill Center for Dance of the New York–based Alvin Ailey American Dance Theater, but mostly on the assumption of a growing middle class that had been promised by civil rights legislation and increased opportunities for Americans of color. The ultimate US state-sponsored affirmation of official culture, the Smithsonian National Museum of African American History and Culture, which opened in 2016, arrives in the wake of the neoliberal economic policies of the 1980s that tilted toward a "solve it yourself" ethos.

But the burgeoning black middle class did not produce a commensurate audience and development base for performance and live art that might be created in response to black life. Neoliberal policies allowed the consolidation of power and resources among a small few that grew smaller between the 1980s and 2000s. The Occupy movement responded to this crisis of a tiny superrich whose influence overwhelms possibilities for others. In the performing arts, consolidation and capitulation to the vagaries of public funding—now privatized—meant the creation of many nostalgia-based, conservative arts companies: the revived Negro Ensemble Company of 2014; the scaled-back Crossroads Theatre Company of New Jersey; the four-production Penumbra Theatre of Saint Paul, Minnesota; and the struggling but still producing Black Rep of St. Louis. Meanwhile, white-led venues, including Berkeley Repertory Theatre, the Alliance Theatre of Atlanta, and Yale Repertory Theatre, continued their practice of including one or two elements of black programming in their annual number. Black venues for performance and black companies shrank and shuttered, falling into configurations that spoke to easily advertised, conservative impulses: theater as achievement-laden history lesson, once-a-year Kwanzaa and black nativity productions, celebrity evenings featuring anecdotal recitations of experiences among the creative class.

The "doing community" gesture of the late twentieth century, which continues in the present, largely failed. Black venues that tried to emulate white venues seldom gathered the local social capital necessary to sustain themselves. Organic communities seldom grew around these venues. As Jean-Luc Nancy has theorized,[1] the "community" cannot be made or coerced; it emerges of its own volition in order to be true to itself and useful in its provocations and achievements. Doing "community outreach" by white institutions for black communities failed because there was no organic need or development of those relationships. Black venues, such as they were, struggled in large part because they had no history to draw on in terms of stable black patronage of the arts; depending on white institutions meant being corralled toward the corner of ethnic work, to be minimized and exoticized as alternative. By the new millennium, a double bind of dysfunctional or nonexistent high-profile black venues or art publics was inevitably tethered to the "one or two artists of color at a time" logic of curation and presenting. By the twenty-first century we wonder, how are we allowing for the emergence of an audience or public of color?

The questions that come to the fore in this awkward detente: Demographics—who participates in art? Social relations—what can art demonstrate to us about one another? Cultural assumptions—how is your art different from mine?

One problem feeding this divide is the pull of the past. Black artistry might produce black publics or assist white audiences in the expansion of their understanding of black lives. But if performance assumed a naturally white art object and a white museum/venue, then black art was often imagined to be a black version of something that could have been white but wasn't in some creative detail, as in a well-made play (about life in an all-black context), an experimental performance (that critiqued stereotypes by leaning into them), a musical with gospel music. We all might have seen or participated in these productions: *A Raisin in the Sun* or *Jar the Floor*, the Broadway production of *The Scottsboro Boys*, *The Gospel at Colonus*. These works engage information about black life and Africanist aesthetics without offering tactics or strategies for enhancing our lives; they offer satisfying diversions. Revolutionary black art, like that of the black arts movement, emerged in black resistance to mainstream scrutiny. Black life has been continually disavowed in the context of the United States; black artistry responds to that disavowal even as demands are made for it to conform to "recognizable" standards of creative exercise.

CURATING FOR COMMUNITIES OF COLOR

In 2015 and 2016, Dasha Chapman, Jane Gabriels, and I cohosted a working group, Configurations in Motion: Performance Curation and Communities of Color, at Duke University in Durham, North Carolina. We wondered, what could happen if we begin our structural wondering about curation from within an assumption of a black, or Latinx, or Native, or Asian American public and the particularities of its assembly and concerns? What if we placed the people who might gather around artistic creativity at the center of the conversation and its conceptualization? What could that shift of focus inspire around the suddenly unavoidable discourses of curatorial practice?

Our call for conference participation wondered, how do we imagine twenty-first-century configurations of performance curation and presenting that acknowledge the particular concerns of audiences and artists of color? How does performance that relates to people of color fit into trends of contemporary curatorial practice? This gathering of presenters, performers, scholars, curators, and managers sought to examine how their work could focus on the involvement, investment, and creative growth of people of color. In a two-day symposium, participants shared their work and insights and produced a gathering of focused thinking about the future of live arts, performance, and the performing arts in the United States, with special attention to black, Caribbean, and Latinx communities.

In 2015 we counted fifteen participants, and in 2016, twenty-one. We asked that the participants arrive ready to engage an "assessment and imagining" workshop. All invitees offered a seven- to ten-minute position paper or brief synopsis of their current work and future goals with regard to the questions posed above. The short symposium convened with all good energy and little agenda, beyond mobilizing our shared interests and achievements, while being attentive to differences in location to the field (however conceived), career, primary areas of expertise and experience, sexuality, geographic location, disability. The convenings held with them an ambition to imagine what a larger structure or future initiatives might be and how they might be nurtured and sustained through time.

The National Museum of African American History and Culture, Washington, DC. Photo: Alan Karchmer, courtesy of National Museum of African American History and Culture

6

The composition of the group mattered to us three conveners. The meetings included artists, curators, funders, presenters, scholars, and community organizers. We counted a majority of stakeholders of color in our grouping and sought to maintain a majority of female-identified voices. Participants offered a mix of scholarly reflection, anecdotal revelations, ambitions, and methodologies for claiming space for communities of color at the center of our curatorial practices. Ultimately, the group confirmed a diversity of approaches to concepts surrounding curation, community, and communities of color.

Moving forward, these sorts of meetings must be commonplace if curating is to become an accepted twenty-first-century art-presenting practice. After all, curators are working in the world and in relation to the varied ways we experience race, culture, gender, sexuality, and class, as well as privilege and comfort; it is crucial for us to consider a variety of approaches toward understanding what live art can do in the world. Curating performance emerges in a world rife with black death and unchecked white patriarchy, the sedimented prison-industrial complex, and generational divergences, including curious baby-boomer senior citizens who know and care about different sorts of things than millennials do. The current international migratory processes demand the address of art-presenting professionals—curators—as they also demand the attention of artists in every mode of performance making. We are commonly compelled to consider art in the world, not just in relationship to itself, and to consider myriad ways to allow live art to emerge in relationship to the lives and loves of people who will experience it. The world and its many concerns must be allowed into the conversations of curatorial practice.

What, then, could our endgame be in these conversations about ethical and engaged curatorial practice? When we talk about *minoritarian art*, we can too easily forget the basic assumptions of *by*, *about*, and *for* that could surround its designation. This might be work that is simultaneously created *by* artists of a particular identity politics but also *about* the imaginative possibilities shared among that group and explicitly made *for* the intellectual expansion of like-identified people who are its primary and particular audience. But so much of the work curated and created by artists of color these days seems mostly to be made not for people but for venues, curators, and critics and an unmarked yet unmistakably white public. Of course, artists need to feel "free" to make whatever we like in response to the world we perceive, or our own imaginations, but we are also quick to bemoan that there are few apparent audiences of color out and about at MOMA, or PS1, or the North Carolina Museum of Art. We create work possibly *about* experiences shared within communities of color but not necessarily *for* them.

The shifting demographics of the United States tell us that white people will no longer be the racial majority in less than thirty years. Alongside that statistic, consider the number of people of color who work as arts administrators. This is a tiny, tiny number. If we have learned anything collectively in our shared work in the arts, it might be that representation matters and that an expanded, diverse field of participants can generate provocative, transformative performance experiences. For now, the shared economy of arts presenting, administration, and funding remains overwhelming and unabashedly white.

We all participate in this "white economy" that elides or overlooks potential minoritarian publics for our creative practices and our curating. When we take a commission from a white venue, or some mainstream black ones, we agree to the long-standing traditions of marginalizing black creativity in relation to its originary communities in order to create work that has the potential to cross over or tour. We need August Wilson to tell stories about us and play on Broadway; we want Bill T. Jones to make work about racism that allows museums and wealthy white audiences to learn about black abjection through dance. But does this work in these venues amplify possibilities for black publics among ourselves?

I'm thinking of the Ralph Lemon series *Some Sweet Day* at MOMA from 2012, in which he famously asked that the commissioned artists address the question, what is black music? Now, this series was in no way conceived as minoritarian art that might be by, about, or for black publics. But it surely seemed to stand in for that sort of gesture by MOMA, and possibly for Lemon. Artists who are commissioned to work outside of their areas of interest, but not necessarily for audiences who are any different from what they might expect, considering the venue at hand, can make work that arrives odd, overwrought, and undercooked. We might remember Deborah Hay's awkward invention for the Lemon series that sparked conversations about curating and communities of color that continued with our gathering at Duke three years later. None of us want to be implicated in using black people as "props" to make art for white people. And yet, crassly, this is what seems to happen far too often when curators commission or present artists of color as part of their series.

Curating, or presenting, is surely a remain of corporatization processes that began to surround the performing arts at the same time that limited but direct government funding for artists became available following the establishment of the National Endowment for the Arts in 1965. The NEA's funding policies essentially ensured that a managerial class of arts presenters would have to be formed in order for the arts to become standardized, as other federally funded projects might be. We can look to the genealogies of several other social programs created in the 1960s, including Community Action against Poverty; these programs required healthy numbers of administrators who could translate ideas from the service providers to the government and those being served. In some ways, curators and presenters might fill a similar function: building connections from artists to audiences and funders.

Today, with that public funding curtailed following Washington's 1980s and 1990s "culture wars," I wonder about a different model of curating and presenting—one that could center its efforts on creating relationships among audiences and sometimes artists. What if the gesture to create community through art were consistently narrated in front of the gesture to secure art and offer it up to an interested (but assumedly ignorant) audience? This is something that dance competitions do, especially the B-girl, house dancing, krumping, and J-Setting battles: communities form around the practice and interest in the arts, and microecologies of celebrity emerge in these contexts. These sorts of arts are not curated as much as administered, and the huge number of people involved in the production of these dance competitions attests to the abiding interest in performance artistry, even if that artistry is couched in the mode of sport. Still, I wonder what would happen if curators focused on creating context for living in the arts by nurturing participation by communities in motion over time. This might be how many artist collectives imagine themselves to work, and how some possibly do function: creating supportive communities of people invested in process together. How could we imagine the action of curating as being directed toward the experience of the so-called audience, participating in the thing that we gather to celebrate/consecrate? Imagining forward, what if entry to the museum could require a drawing, and entry to a performance could require a dance?

Let's take a moment to spin here in directions that have already been tried in high-profile "white" contexts, such as in the *Move: Choreographing You* exhibit in London[2] and in several of Tino Sehgal's "constructed situation" works, including *This Progress*. Of course, even as they encourage participation, these works assume an intractable separation of artist and audience or viewer/witness/participant. The direct address of the work is simulated; the works do not change, given varied responses by communities of audience, and the audience is designated to be responsible for its own experience within the work, whether good, bad, or indifferent. I wonder, what if we were to put our faith in the allowance for relationship in community and direct our energy toward what people in that community actually value as engaged art practice; we might come up with models that service and inspire communities of color in unexpected ways. For example, the Philadelphia project that the Pew Center for Arts and Heritage and the Painted Bride Art Center have launched casts around the places that Philadelphians hold dear to their sense of its history; those unusual, neglected places become the site of performance but also an occasion to remember place differently. Because it is the Bride, the artists and consultants to the project are mostly black people, and the fantasy of the project as an in-reach rather than an out-reach sort of site-specific exercise is to engage black communities around sustained experiences of art making—making art inside the geographic communities rather than making art and out-reaching it to the presumed communities. This could be something similar the Institute on the Arts and Civic Dialogue that Anna Deavere Smith founded and ran at Harvard University, with its engaged core audience group that participated the entire three years of its existence there in the late 1990s.

Participatory work such as Sehgal's tends to lead to discussions of deskilling and concerns about the usurping of performance expertise—technique and virtuosity—as hallmarks of art making. The question might become, are we just talking about process-based materials that involve the audience as art makers? I am not sure about this, but I do wonder about recentering communities in formation, not as recipients of "great art" that is found and offered up by an expert broker/impresario but as the focus of the live art experience as it might be conceived by that middle-management position. Encouraging the community to engage its dormant creativities might be what curators explore. Some curators certainly take on these tasks, even as they work in sideward, small venues or circumstances that will seldom land them in the pages of the *New Yorker*, if that were their goal. These curators might define themselves as social architects or social sculptors; they might be activists affiliated with Black Lives Matter who do indeed attend experimental performance events and ask pointed questions about working with artists who present imaginative, provocative work. As an example, at the *afroFUTUREqu##r* platform staged at JACK in Brooklyn, New York, on October 15–18, 2015, co-curated by myself with Niv Acosta; two members of Black Lives Matter Philadelphia attended the Sunday brunch panel "*afroFUTUREqu##r*: Black Art, White Venues, and the New Black Presence in Elite Performance." These artist-curator-activists brought a clarity of intention that surrounded their mission to encourage live art for the urgent social justice movement into the space of New York experimental performance. Like others working to create performance experiences with spiritual, sensual, gender nonnormative, or living folkways traditions, curators can begin with a need to create particular space for people who are not finding that live art regularly or reliably attends to their imaginative concerns.

In terms of creative work, though, and lining up my own interests in the archive and technology that is always already surrounding us, and in performance as a singularity that might be available to communities in motion, I want to share a SLIPPAGE project in development: the video "The Weight of Ideas."[3] This interface allows the movement of the performer to manipulate identity labels that are projected onto a screen behind

Faustin Linyekula's *Philly Files*, the Painted Bride, Philadelphia, 2016. Photo: Kristel Baldoz

the performer. This interface also can be used for performance, as it is in this video, but we also strive to create a version that allows audiences to decide the words they want to "tether" to their body and the music that they want to hear as they work, physically, inside the interface. Like many SLIPPAGE creations, the interface requires the input of the participant to activate it; these creations intend to be immediate-gratification sorts of devices that value our own movement among an archive of ideas to create their effect. An ambition for SLIPPAGE is to create these sorts of devices that will allow for group communion, rather than only for solo performance structures that rely on a silent and still audience.

But talking about curating is not the same as talking about making art. Somehow, I do want to get away from the focus on the artist or the artwork/performance as the measure of artistic experience and the thing that needs to be protected or enhanced by curators. I believe there are other possibilities for live art and performance, and I want to imagine giving that power to the people.

Curating, as it is widely understood now, seems to me middle-management work and as such might be greatly enhanced by placing emphasis on its stakeholders. Granted, the possibilities for live art surely need to be protected, and maybe curators are people who do that. But I have not really noticed that live art might be endangered, especially in contexts like MOMA or PS1, while I have wondered at the curation or creation of varied publics to experience performance. It seems a shame to me that we might create new structures that value the act of curating as art practice over the need to develop strategies to allow for direct participation in the arts by, about, and for the people (whomever they might be). White publics that are hipsterish, or art-school-ish, ivy-league-ish, middle-aged executive, straightish, or retired-curious still tend to go unidentified and assumed as the foundational audiences for our curatorial exercises, even when we work in places where that is not the majority population that might participate in the events we create. What if we actually sought to create counterpublics or particular publics that could make manifest possibilities for performance that are not simply slotted into season-driven planning?

Artists will continue to make unexpected work, and there will always be space for the unexpected, unanticipated performance that requires everyone to witness in stillness and reflection for a bit of time while something that has been rehearsed unfolds. But maybe curatorial process could be less concerned about protecting that possibility and more concerned with the social engineering necessary for a community to recognize itself as stakeholders in the process, or venue, where art emerges.

For me, this is more like the endgame of curating: to create possibilities for artists and publics to emerge where they were not visible to each other before. The usual suspects of publics for live art and dance performance we know; where are the queer black communities invigorated by curators intent on commissioning and presenting work by queer black artists? Are we working simultaneously to allow the emergence of public discourse that is actually for a particular public? It seems so easy to get to the *by* and *about* portions of minoritarian art and its presenting, but the *for* portion of the equation calls for the development of trust and communication that arrive rarely among professional curators.

Ultimately, I do think of curating as something like social engineering, rather than its own art practice, in no small part because of its emergence as a managerial practice, in the middle (somewhat elevated), that intends to create context for the urgent encounters with unexpected expertise—or art—that we all desperately need.

CENTERING THE PEOPLE RATHER THAN THE OBJECTS: THE COMMONS

Contemporary social theory has created a category of the "commons" to describe the assembly of people toward group relationship that aligns contingent interests and needs. The commons emerges to be different from sedimented concepts of community; the commons imagines itself to be contingent and ephemeral, momentary but stable in some ways, like the "thousand plateaus" of Gilles Deleuze and Félix Guattari.[4] The commons recognizes itself briefly and then moves away from itself, leaving traces of its achievement in Black Lives Matter, in the Occupy movement, in student uprisings against gun access and LGBTQ hate crimes. The commons is wiser than the individuals that comprise it, because it values the sensibility of the group. It is not bound by class or strict demographics, because it emerges as an aspirational, ideological space of exchange. The commons tends to imagine and form itself as the subaltern who have not spoken, or the abject 99 percent who have little voice in public policy. The com-

Video still of Thomas F. DeFrantz and Kenneth David Steward's *The Weight of Ideas*, Duke University, Durham, NC, 2015. Photo courtesy of the artist

mons might make space for those culture workers already engaged in the labor of presenting or curating, but it certainly forms around emergent voices and ideologies of change; it imagines newly reconstituted publics and creative makers/artists.

Considering a commons at the center of curatorial discourse could possibly help us all. In the commons, how we respond to creative craft and production matters, possibly more than the fact of creative craft. *That* we respond in the commons matters more than *how*. Art does not have to make us feel good in some way, or tell us things we already know, but it might want to encourage us to recognize ourselves rather than the historical legacies of its own production.

If curation is something like social engineering, then its materials include its context and its stakeholders. Typically, that context is conceived as background: we imagine the series, and then we try to figure out how to get an audience in the room. But what if we started with the people who might want to be in the room? What if we imagined the audience as the reason to become an engineer, in the way that people design bridges to help others get from one place to another. Of course, the best engineers pay attention to questions of who, what, where, when, and why before they start asking questions of how. As curators, where do we begin? Well, we believe in art, because we know it contains healing and rejuvenating imaginative possibilities; we want people to have access to a nondenominational imaginative healing.

This calls for us to resist thinking of the context for performance or art being their own histories. In the visual arts this would be impossible; logics of visual arts are always about the relationship of the emergent to the previous—we cannot have suprematism without futurism, or pointillism without impressionism. Dance and live performance might be a little bit different from this, in that while we turn to Katherine Dunham, Pearl Primus, or Alvin Ailey to confirm that we have ancestors, and we celebrate Gus Solomons Jr. or Blondell Cummings for their persistence as experimental artists, we make new work because we have to, in response to the present moment. Performance is not only about itself and its own history but also about the relationships that grow up around the possibilities of its execution—the relationships among collaborators and funders and presenters. But what if we start with the commons or audience with whom the work is shared? As social engineers, what if we stay in the place where we prioritize the needs or ambitions of the community that emerges around it? And if we want the sites of performance to feel like they value the needs and aspirations of black people, we might want to start by figuring out how to construct those spaces: what they look like, what they feel like, how they have been constructed, and what they do.

This inversion might feel far away from the action of curation that we might aspire to in our quests for power or taste making. But we have inspiration in the black arts movement, which had such great impact in large part because it emerged from the needs of the community that responded to it; those who were enlivened and enraged by it grew in its presence. When we mythologize that brief moment in creative time now, we talk about how it was created around people; it was art that responded to the moment and the population that encircled it.

So our strategies today could be based in big data, or in experiential knowledges, or in relationships and friendships that we develop along the way. We could leverage social media to examine data about where communities convene and create circumstances that speak to what is missing from those profiles. We can start social activist performance venues in places where we know that people need an opportunity to express, as many of us do already, because we experientially know when and where to enter. Or we can create alliances that allow us to listen and learn, through time, toward a possibility of embedded action and building.

This could be the endgame for us all, then: to imagine creative exchange that considers our assembly, and temporary recognition across difference, as the reason to participate in art—by, about, and for an us briefly convened but sparkling in discovery rather than abject solitude or misrecognitions. Let us make space for one another, by retreating from having to know what's next or what came before and instead encouraging a long-winded encounter of an art making public with itself.

Notes

1. Jean-Luc Nancy, *The Inoperative Community*, ed. Peter Connor, trans. Peter Cooper, Lisa Garbus, Michael Holland, and Simona Sawhney (Minneapolis: University of Minnesota Press, 1991).

2. *Move: Choreographing You*, Southbank Centre, London, 2010, move.southbankcentre .co.uk/microsite/.

3. Thomas F. DeFrantz and Kenneth David Steward, "The Weight of Ideas," January 5, 2015, SLIPPAGE: Performance, Culture, Technology, www.youtube.com/watch?v=vqzy _Ay2tTI.

4. Gilles Deleuze and Felix Guattari, *A Thousand Plateaus: Capitalism and Schizophrenia*, trans. Brian Massumi (Minneapolis: University of Minnesota Press, 1987).

Artists Organisations
International, initiated by
Florian Malzacher, Jonas
Staal, and Joanna Warsza;
Block I, Propaganda &
Counter Propaganda:
Concerned Artists of the
Philippines (Lisa Ito), HAU,
Berlin, 2015.
Photo: Lidia Rossner

Agonism and the Next Word

Florian Malzacher

Interviewed by Tom Sellar

Critic, dramaturg, and curator Florian Mal-
zacher currently serves as curator and artistic
director of the Impulse Theater Festival in Düs-
seldorf, Cologne, and Mülheim, Germany. His
2012 convening "Truth Is Concrete," a 24/7 mara-
thon "camp" under the auspices of the festival Stei-
rischer Herbst in Graz, Austria, considered tactics
and priorities for art and social engagement. (A
corresponding 2014 anthology with the same title
has been published by Sternberg Press.) I spoke
with Malzacher in Mülheim in June 2015 during
Impulse's month-long exploration of "theater as
agonistic space, in which social and political dif-
ferences can be openly negotiated"—a curatorial
frame inspired in part by the political theory of
Chantal Mouffe. We began by discussing the recent
proliferation of the term curation *in a performing*
arts context.—TS

FLORIAN MALZACHER I don't often see that
many interesting curatorial projects. Maybe
there are some, and maybe there are beginning to be more. But sometimes I have the
feeling that it's already considered enough to
say, that's curatorial, and then not to do anything differently.

Is *curator* the best term to take over?
What does it mean to take it from the visual
arts and use it for the performing arts? Is it a

good idea or not? I was always fine with using
this term as a provocation. A provocation, on
one side, to a certain practice of programming
that exists: to say, you need to accelerate it,
to enhance it, to push it somewhere. On the
other hand, it's also a self-provocation: if you
call yourself a curator instead of a programmer, you have to deliver. Or else, someone
could say to you, why are you doing this? For
me, the term is only interesting because it
demands something. It's a demand to persons
calling themselves a curator. In this regard,
when the term *curator* is just used affirmatively, then I'm not interested. In that case,
we already need the next term. If we just
exchange one word for another and are satisfied with what we are doing, then it's useless.
We should probably think, is this really a good
term? If it's just a new name for something
that was called something different before,
that's fine, we can do that. But it's not really
interesting. It's only interesting if it demands a
different concept.

TOM SELLAR *What's exciting about curation is*
the idea of that expanded role, and the idea of the
transformation for theater, specifically, that could
come with it—that there could be linkages between
individual performances and between artistic

Theater 47:1   DOI 10.1215/01610775-3710520
© 2017 by Tom Sellar

Chantal Mouffe's *Radical Democracy and Agonistic Politics*, Impulse Theater Festival, Düsseldorf, 2015. Photo: Sandra Körmann

projects, which is so lacking within institutional structures right now. It carries the promise that somebody could begin to make connections, to create contexts, and also to generate a kind of research engine for the theater that doesn't exist today. It could be linked to what Beatrice von Bismarck calls the "cultures of the curatorial," as opposed to the "practice" of curating. It encompasses the larger idea of a knowledge base that each project builds on, adding historical linkages and also contemporary linkages, keeping track of what's been attempted before or what's being attempted now. It would ask, how does each project contribute to some kind of investigation that would further the curatorial discovery? This happens, in theory, in the art world as well. That seems to be the curatorial function that would be really essential for a contemporary theater. Do you agree?

This is exactly the point: to have a field, to create a field within the festival, or program, or performative conference, to create this field where the curatorial, as Beatrice von Bismarck called it, could happen. But then the question would be, what is specific for theater in this? Curators also need to raise this question: what could be the performative in curation? How is the situation that you curate performative in itself? That would be interesting for me. One can use theatrical expertise in curating something—and I don't mean that you need

a set design that shows can happen in—but one can think of how bodies move and how time passes. I don't mean "theatrical" in a cheesy way. Hannah Hurtzig has a very clear set design for what she does. Hers is a curatorial project that becomes an artwork, almost. That's also possible.

For me, I want to ask, what does it mean when we spend time together? Can we enforce this? With a festival like the Impulse Theater Festival, you work within a largely normal festival rhythm. People come for a weekend and then they leave. It's different with something like Artist Organisations International, or "Truth Is Concrete," which lasted 170 hours. When you invite people to stay for that amount of time, you have to think about what time means. What does it mean when people spend time together, when they become a collective? When they get annoyed with each other? What group dynamics kick in? That's what I think is specific for the field of theater in the practice of curation. A performance is already a curated event, in a way. You invite people. You might have a narrative. You have sounds; you think of the space; you think of how the audience comes in. If you think of theater as a public space, where society can meet and also define itself and experiment with its procedures, how can you enlarge this space for a bigger program? Thinking from the specificities of theater itself—that's the interesting part.

You're one of the only curators in a theater context who talks about time. You build experiments with time into the structure and the fabric of your projects. "Truth Is Concrete" was a 24/7 marathon, where you could feel time changing, speeding up, and slowing down, and even the time between performances, riding the bus, was another journey, another dialogue, another opportunity for exchange. Time is obviously what sets theater apart from the visual arts.

My interest in time comes directly from what theater does. One major difference between theater and the visual arts—normally, but with many exceptions—is that, when you go to the show, you have to spend your time in there. You force people, in a very anachronistic way, to sit three hours at a show, or even only for ninety minutes. People from within the visual arts often think that's strange.

I think that's why Dorothea von Hantelmann says, for her, a museum feels much more contemporary than a theater, because you're not forced into time frames. I would also say that that's the neoliberal aspect of the museum, if you want to call it that. Theater forces you to stay, most of the time. If you decide you have to leave, it might be unpleasant. People notice it. There are shows where you can go in and out, but more often the expectation is that you stay for that time. You have to make a commitment in terms of time. I think, with all our schedules now and how life runs, to make a commitment of time is actually one of the biggest commitments you can make. If I commit to a show for ninety minutes, or for three hours, or for five hours, or for twelve hours, it's really a commitment. That's something to think about: What happens when you make this commitment? What can you do? What can you experience, then, and how can you change atmospheres and intensities? I found time always interesting within shows. In Forced Entertainment's twelve-hour shows, which they did in Germany, you spent five hours watching people walking in a circle. All these things happen when you give in to that and say to yourself, "I know nothing will happen anymore." In a time-based art you have to ask: How can I use this? How can I play with this?

When you do something nonstop for a week, which means people will sleep and people will go in and out, it also means that you will create a group dynamic. In the middle of the week, there will be a crisis, and suddenly this becomes part of the program. It's actually kind of predictable. Groups are not so surprising. Even if you say your performance is only an hour, you can work with time's limits. I think curating, in a way, is about wanting to control something that you can't control. You have a plan, and you really want to follow it, but you have to be aware that it will not happen. That's the fun of it. Curating is a cure for control freaks, basically, but you have to be a control freak to want to do it. This is also what the theater that I'm interested in is about.

You've centered the 2015 Impulse Theater Festival on two questions. One concerns agonistic pluralism, and the other probes the limits of representation and what those limits mean politically. How long have you been thinking about these questions in these terms, and when did you decide that they were right for this season's program?

Impulse is less a curated event, and so I try to approach it from this view. It's a festival with a tradition and a certain task. It's not a twenty-four-hour event. Impulse invites shows and builds something around it with them. I kind of like Impulse, because most of the curatorial work that we do does not market a specific program. At Impulse, we invite shows to perform. Then, we have an audience, and we need to deal with that. It's much less focused on one clear curatorial concept. For us, it was very interesting to see what concepts did emerge. I think a lot of artists at the moment are dealing with how they can relate to the political situations around us, which don't seem to be getting better. So there's a big need for a lot of theater makers and a lot of other artists to deal with the realities around them and maybe even to intervene. Their question is, what could be the role of theater within this? What could a political theater be? What could theater as a social place be? That is something that a lot of artists are dealing with and that we are also interested in. It's a focus that came about very organically, because I think it's happening in the world. There's a search—maybe it's more of an ongoing search for what political theater and theater as a public space could be, today, than questions with very clear answers.

Thinking about all this in relation to the curatorial, as Beatrice von Bismarck defines it, we also came to like Chantal Mouffe's notion of agonism. It's likely we're misusing this concept, which always happens when you draw a political or a philosophical concept into art. That's fine. Mouffe uses a term that comes from theater—*agon*, of course, is the competition of arguments in a Greek drama. What she argues against—I simplify this, of course—is the idea that we need to try to reach consensus, or that society, ultimately, in a Marxist ideology or otherwise, would lead to consensus in a better world or in hundreds of years we could reach consensus. She, like others, argues that there will never be consensus. There will always be different positions. Rather, we have to find a way of making these differences visible and to create an *agon* between ideas. Otherwise, the impossible struggle for consensus will lead to antagonism and to clashes of ideas and to war; one encounters opinions that cannot even have a dialogue with one another anymore. I think that's quite a good description of what's happening in the world, in many different places. Germany is very much on the path of consensus, but you can see that it's not functioning politically in different corners. From a distance, it seems that the United States is very much going in the direction of antagonism, where you have divides between opinions that can no longer be bridged.

We found this idea of agonism quite interesting, because it has always been the function of theater, from the Greeks on. Theater brought together these different opinions and had the audience negotiate them. This is our idea—that the festival is, in a way, an agonistic field. It doesn't pretend to present *everything*—I also find work that I think would be horrible, even to have this opinion expressed—but within the agonistic field of the festival, I have the feeling that there's a negotiation of topics, of society and politics, that can still communicate with each other across differences. We tried to create a field where this could happen. Theater is a good place for agonism, because theater has a paradoxical construction: you are in the artwork as an audience member, and, at the same time, you can watch yourself from without, but not by distancing yourself from what's happening, not by moving *out*. I think of the image in the movies, when you die or when you're in a coma, and you suddenly watch yourself from above—an out-of-body experience. That's the image I have of what theater does.

We had conversations that one could call a kind of therapy. Since it is theater and you're aware of yourself within it, you can analyze the situation. You're in and out at the same moment. That's what theater can do very well—better than a complete identification with a character, which in film functions much more successfully. That doesn't function well for me in theater. What functions in theater is this swimming, in and out—going from being part of it to analyzing it from without. I use this function to look at what theater can be today, in society.

I was thinking as I participated in the Dutch theater maker Lotte van den Berg's facilitated group conversation that it is a lot easier to create agonism among all white people between the ages of thirty and fifty, who share similar politics. Although I did feel particularly American during the conversation about migration: I suddenly became aware of the discrepancies between our discourses in America and Europe—a relatively small difference within the West. There were no Turkish or Syrian people

Gob Squad's
Western Society,
Impulse Theater
Festival, Mülheim
an der Ruhr, 2015.
Photo:
Robin Junicke

*in the workshop, for example. How do you make
sure that these performances actually cause a disruption? And if they did cause a disruption, isn't
that at odds with the mission of the festival, which
is about harmony and creating an enjoyable,
municipal event? Isn't agonism at odds with the
institution of the Impulse Theater Festival?*

A festival like Impulse is much more com-
promised in terms of curatorial ideas—which
is sort of nice. I'm not against it. I think that
compromise is something else that is very specific to theater, and I don't think it's necessarily a negative.

 I think that Joanna Warsza and I created a much more agonistic space at Artist Organisations International, which was
also much more diverse in its participation.
But it was a clearly curatorial event. There,
we had two acts from the Artist Association
of Azawad, and we had Kurdish representatives and we had white, middle-class artists
from wherever. But the agenda was never
one of reconciliation. We carried on conten-
tious discussions, for three days, each lasting
until early morning, but nobody left, because

there was still a field to bring people together.
Everybody was interested in staying and not
leaving. The impulse to stay was not simply to
not yield the field to the others but rather to
continue the discussion. That, perhaps, would
be a much better example of agonism.

 Impulse, of course, needs more local
support. It alternates between three cities, but
only two of them are big cities—Düsseldorf
and Cologne—while Mülheim is a small city.
Impulse needs to create an audience in a city
that is not used to this kind of theater. I totally
agree that the curatorial mission is compro-
mised in this regard.

 In terms of who is represented, that's
one of the questions that we're trying to ask
in this festival. The questions of who is representing whom, and what right they have to
represent the other, who is not represented—
these are core questions of democracies. And
these are the core questions of theater, always.
While this idea that theater has always been
related to democracy is already perhaps banal,
it's interesting to remind oneself of this when
considering why theater is a good place to ask
these questions. Especially in Germany, as in

Gintersdorfer/
Klaßen's *Das Neue
Schwarze Denken—
Chefferie*, Impulse
Theater Festival,
Mülheim an der
Ruhr, 2015. Photo:
Robin Junicke

many European countries, we have a problem of representation. There is a very limited representation, not only onstage but also in our audiences, of people that are not white and middle class. But the problem of representation is also a problem of our society, and something that is heavily discussed both in society and in theater lately.

I would say that Germany has been late to some of these discussions, because our colonial past was always eclipsed by other things to come afterward, which occupied us more. The colonial period was a short period in German history. The time of straightforward colonialism ended after the First World War, and it started late. I don't mean this cynically, but German colonialism was less brutal than the Belgian, so we didn't feel the need to think much about it. When you look at German cities, at the presence of non-European foreigners or migrants, one understands that, until now, this diversity was never very present. You would not see many black people or Asian people in the streets. It changes now, and there's an urge to understand problems of representation, especially with regard to the Turkish people, who were once the biggest group of workers migrating to Germany. We are very late to that discussion.

For this reason, many of these discourses are seemingly naive from the outside. But it's a big topic, and I think we can begin by simply raising the question. We are asking for that. We point at it. Even if you have a show with a nondiverse group of western European people in the audience or onstage, you can make this lack visible. It's not true that this is always the case, but of course in many shows it is. I think the first step is to be aware of it. I cannot change the world with one festival, but we try to have works that function in this way or function differently.

My best example of this would be Gob Squad's production *Western Society*. Gob Squad does what they always do: they play themselves. This was a politically aware step to take in the nineties, when artists began to realize that they cannot talk about others, as all the city theaters do and all the repertory theaters did. We had to talk about ourselves, because that was the only thing we really knew something about. Over the years, that gesture becomes self-referential and loses its initial impetus of social and political awareness. To address this, Gob Squad doesn't stop playing themselves, but suddenly their show is called *Western Society*. What happened was, suddenly, they realized that they had both to show themselves and to acknowledge that they are not everything, that they are just this little part of humanity. The whole show is very nostalgic about a society that actually doesn't seem to exist anymore or maybe it shouldn't exist anymore.

Western Society *exudes contemporaneity because it shows the ways we project ourselves or insert ourselves into images that we take from the Other. In the show, we see a mysterious YouTube video and we know nothing about the people in it. All we can do is imagine them and to put ourselves inside this frame where there is no Other, only pure subjectivity.*

Yes, definitely. For me, within the work of Gob Squad that represents themselves all the time, or presents representations of themselves all the time, this was an interesting step. It functioned almost like a telescope. If you turn a telescope in a different way and look through the wrong end, suddenly you feel as if the very close is very far away at the same moment. This is one thing we can show in the theater, that the *we* that we represent is just this little part of the world. The most opposite gesture from that, within a German or a western European context, would be the work of Gintersdorfer/Klaßen. It's unusual work, since for more than ten years they have been working together with performers from outside of the West—first from the Ivory Coast and later with performers from Rwanda, the Congo, and other African countries. More and more, Gintersdorfer/Klaßen withdrew as directors, and more and more they handed over the stage to their performers. The piece that we show at Impulse is called *Chefferie*. It stages the idea of a system where everyone is a chief, and equal chiefs negotiate what is to be done. What they represent is actually the system of how they create work. They have a lot of equal chiefs involved in each project. That

may be a different approach to self-referential representation than Gob Squad uses.

We are also showing a work by director Milo Rau, who is in a way maybe the most conventional theater director within the context of Impulse, because he usually works with actors, who play roles. Rau deals with humanitarian crimes in his work. *Hate Radio*, for example, was about atrocities in Rwanda. Rau had the idea to go with his actors and to do research in Brussels about the young kids that joined the jihad or pledged to ISIS. Suddenly, they kind of realized that this was not possible. They could not represent this idea. They couldn't get close to that. The work shifted, and now the actors talk about their own lives and their own moments of possible political radicalization. They talk about their relationships with their fathers. They talk about Western society, once again. They look for what is happening within their own expertise. In a way, in this work Rau makes the same shift that Gob Squad did years before. It's a rotation of the idea of how representation can function.

The Lebanese artist Rabih Mroué, too, who presented his work *Riding on a Cloud*, always talks about representation in a personal and poetic way. He brings his brother Yasser onstage, who literally cannot understand representation. He was shot, as a kid, in the civil war in Beirut, and has a syndrome that makes it impossible for him to recognize reality in words and pictures. He would understand a cup of coffee, but when looking at a photo of a cup of coffee he could not recognize it. He really truly doesn't understand the function of representation or what representation is.

So I think what we try to show is how representation functions or doesn't function. That's a huge question, of course, in theater but also in society. There are people who say they want to get to a postrepresentational

Ahmet Ögüt's
*The Silent University
Ruhr*, Impulse
Theater Festival,
Mülheim an der
Ruhr, 2015. Photo:
Robin Junicke

society, that representation is not a good way to build a society. Chantal Mouffe would always defend representation, but also questions how representation functions. In theater, we ask: Is it okay to represent other characters? When is it not okay? Germany is having a big debate about blackface in theater, which is quite interesting.

This is following a controversy over a poster advertising a production that used blackface.

Yes, directed by Johan Simons, but there are also many others. It's a big topic because, of course, it leads to a sequence of the questions. You begin by confirming that, as a white actor, I'm not supposed to play a black actor. The next question you ask is, as a white actor, how am I supposed to play another white person that's not me? Suddenly, you find yourself at the borders of acting. The questions of theater and the questions of society immediately overlap.

That was evident in the Chefferie *performance last night. There is a kind of chaos that is always threatening to erupt when somebody begins to speak for someone else or when it's not clear which language is supposed to be spoken.*

It was an interesting moment, because the show was announced as the English version of the show, but some people in the show didn't understand that, so they only spoke German. There was also a show where everything was translated from French into English but not into German. The actor that was German, the one actor that was German and who speaks German, began to deliver a speech about inclusion and critical whiteness in German, and at the exact same moment excluded all the non-German speaking audience. And then, he realized this.

He even excluded his fellow performers, who didn't understand what was happening onstage. It was amazing.

Exactly. I liked this moment, because it really made the problems clear.

There was a genuine sensation of vertigo. You didn't know which way it was going to go, which was kind of exciting. Then there's the other side of representation, political representation: Who is here? Who is invited? Is there a need to curate a public, as well as a program?

That would be the question of audience development, which is also a political question. I think we all agree that we'd like to have a big and very diverse audience and wonder how we reach it—that for me is a less interesting question. I think, as a provocation, one should think of how we can build a different audience in terms of how it would make sense to make work for this audience. We will not solve in one theater festival, or even in theater in general, all of the problems of society. We are part of this problem of society and represent it, to a certain degree. If we recognize this and would like to have different conversations, how can we work to do that?

You hope, over the years, that audience diversity will improve in the rest of the festival or through other kinds of work that you can begin to add after a festival has become an institution. However, a more interesting idea demands that you open the festival to a different audience by changing the rules of the festival itself. Interestingly enough, changing the rules seems to build a higher threshold to involvement, rather than a lower one.

Impulse hosted a project called the Silent University, which was originally initiated by Ahmet Öğüt, a Kurdish visual artist, first at the Tate Modern and then at Tensta Konsthall, as well as one in Hamburg and one here in Düsseldorf. The Silent University is a self-organized, open university, where the teachers are academics that came to Germany as refugees or asylum seekers. They don't have working permits here, or their degrees are not convertible or not accepted here, or they can't find, for other reasons, opportunities to teach. The Silent University is not addressing itself at all to the audience of the festival. This is a long-term project, which we can guarantee for three years. But it should last, of course, forever. A completely different audience comes to the Silent University, and it will be interesting to see whether or not it stays a completely different audience. For a project like that, the

curators move out of our field completely and hand it over to others and to the artist. Then, after the project has completed, we see if there is an interest for that side to return to their connection with us.

I like the idea of curating audiences, because it's a challenge and it's also a self-provocation, again. If you do curate an audience, there's a hierarchy. I think it's something interesting to play with that can help us analyze the situation we are in.

It seems clear that we can no longer leave audience development to the education department of a performing arts organization that traditionally would call a few school groups and invite them to the performance. That seems insufficient, given the crises that these organizations and institutions are in now, and the pressure they are under to demonstrate their wider reach. Audience development has to become more central to their programming focus.

My Yale colleague Michael Warner has written a book, Publics and Counterpublics, *about the notion of the public now. Whereas once we could presume that theater spoke to a monolithic public, he argues—speaking not of theater but of political discourse in general—that the public is today composed of micropublics. Micropublics form around specific discourses and specific events that attract interested people in the way that a thread does on social media. Discourse becomes a little cluster of voices formed around that particular conversation. Perhaps our projects need to think of themselves as doing the same thing.*

The idea that there is not one society, that this concept does not work anymore, is a big discussion among all the city theaters here. On the one hand, I totally agree, and on the other hand, I've been thinking lately that maybe it's not true. Looking at, if not last month's then last year's shows, I wonder if the idea of classes is more persistent than we thought. They may change, and perhaps there is no longer a working class in many countries where there used to be, but at the same time a different kind of working class emerges. I think we are witnessing a rise of the bourgeoisie again not only in economic terms but also in terms of the idea of education and the German idea of *Bildung*, of self-cultivation through education. Maybe there are still more persistent publics that exist.

Another problem that arises around micropublics is how to avoid the trap of the project. I have a feeling that there's a big wish within the arts at the moment to get away from the extremely dominant model of the project, which has enabled a lot of creativity, because it's a flexible model. However, it's not sustainable. There's a big debate in Germany about how much project work and independent theater are actually behind the rise of neoliberalism in theater. They adhere to the best neoliberal model: artists make work for and from very little money, they make something out of everything, and, once they're done, you can get rid of them immediately.

How, then, can one develop a project that is sustainable? The fact that more and more artistic groups and also individual projects take the name and often the structure of institutions and organizations is an interesting symptom. You can very clearly see that there seems to be an interest in more sustainable models, and perhaps in re-institutionalizing, albeit in a different way and towards what could be a different kind of an institution. The notion of an institution or an organization is not seen negatively anymore, as I think it was for a long time. In this festival alone, we have Milo Rau with the Institute for Political Murder, an institute. We have a project that translates to *The Institution*, by Herbordt/Mohren, *Die Aufführung*. There are already two things, by chance, that take the name, at least, of an organizational institution. We didn't choose them for that reason, either, and I could continue with this list.

Ahmet Öğüt always said of the Silent University that it should never be referred to as a project. This is not a project. It is a university. It's an institution. It's an organization, and this is an important distinction.

Yes, on the one hand, we have to very clearly target very different groups, and, on the other hand, we still find common interests that unite a lot of people. There are still certain class differences that exist and are maybe growing at the moment. But there is also more and more consensus growing—although I shouldn't say that word. For years, we were in the situation where everyone would say that ideologies no longer function, but now there's an interest in finding common ground, getting out of the trap of complete contingency and relativism.

I wonder how we will do that.

I wonder too.

It sounds utopian.

If theater is a good tool for searching and looking for answers, then I sense that there has been a shift in what is being looked for. I don't know what it will lead to. In ten years we will know: Was this in vain? Did something come out of it?

That's why theater still matters, perhaps. It has the capacity to create temporary social experiments where we can see what works and what doesn't. Most of them don't work, but we gain something from the few that do.

Since the beginning, I think, theater has been the best art form for trying out the procedures of society, for inventing new procedures, and for testing or for failing with them. It's the field where that still can function, if you use it for that.

You're still someone who believes in the radical potential of new artistic practices. The book that you published, Truth Is Concrete, *is an example of that. It's a book of possible strategies. More cynical people look at the cultural industry and see its infinite neoliberal ability to absorb radical practices and turn them into products, but you don't look at art that way.*

Of course, that is always possible, and that is part of society. But where else, beyond theater, would you have these possibilities? I'm not idealizing it, but I think that if there is still a place where you can have some radical imagination, it's in this field. Fortunately, theater is much less driven by a high-speed market than the visual arts. It's an old-fashioned tool. It's slow. You can't really sell it well. The people who do it are old-fashioned and nerdy. It's much less sexy than visual art in many ways, and much less a part of the market. The paradox of visual art is that it's the place where a lot of radical critical thinking is being developed, at the same time as it is the most neoliberal market. That's an interesting paradox. The theater has these problems as well but not in the same way. Theater is still difficult to place in the market, but it's still a part of it. We are still a part of it. I'm not arguing for an idealized view of art or saying that theater is an exception. It's not. But if there are still places where you can create a public sphere, I think that art should be used for that. That's more my point—whether you're working in visual art or wherever, if you can still make use of your resources on behalf of society, then you have to do it. You cannot say that theater's a great place and art's not. No, no. If anything, anywhere has this possibility, we have the obligation to make use of it.

That's a lot of pathos for this early morning conversation.

Milo Rau's
The Civil Wars,
Impulse Theater
Festival, Mülheim
an der Ruhr, 2015.
Photo:
Sandra Körmann

I wanted to ask you about an article you recently wrote in which you said that, at the moment, the field is still dominated by transition models.[1] You were talking specifically about the generation of professionals that started the Kunsthalles in the 1980s and 1990s. The founders were subsequently replaced by their apprentice-successors, but today that means that those institutions are still searching for new evolutionary strategies. Can you talk more about what those organizations might be transitioning to? Is the festival structure going to endure? Could we be moving to some other structure that can accommodate the kind of independent groups that you describe, who are turning themselves into little, self-sufficient units, who then negotiate with producers and presenters? Is there something other than a presenting model that could work?

27

I think still the utopian ideal behind the Kunstencentrum, for example, which probably they achieved, is still functioning. If you are looking for a house that can at one moment be very flexible and accommodate projects that turn over quickly, and at the same time enables sustainability and continuation, one that not only presents work but brings it into a dialogue for an audience, I think that's still something that is needed. That exists almost nowhere, for different reasons. The places in the United States that come closest to satisfying this need don't have any money to do anything, and they rely on sponsors and donors. There are two or three handfuls of houses in the whole of Europe like that, and most of them don't have the opportunities to really do work well. In these cases, the project becomes a pragmatic tool, because that's the only kind of work you can realize. You mount festivals, because you can apply for money for them. Money plays a role in what models you use to present. We need to create the possibility of an institution that stays in transition, that continually tries to follow up and develop itself. That's the struggle, to ask how this could be possible. Can it be possible? How can it, because as soon as you institutionalize yourself, you have to shift again, and after you become an institution, you face pragmatic limits that make things get stuck immediately. Is it possible to find an institution in permanent transition? That's a Leninist idea—permanent revolution.

And we know what happened there.

I think at the moment there's a shift in perception. It's more and more clear that it's not good to get rid of all institutions and to be against institutions per se. We can be happy that we still have some institutions, but we have to see how we can transform them while they're still running, in order not to lose them. In these economical and ideological crises that you see in Europe, you see countries like Germany, that have been building up institutions for a long time, so that even if the state gets dismantled, they still have some institutions left. In eastern Europe, however, where institutions in many countries were not even built, it's much more difficult to construct them—but that's very abstract. I think the challenge of creating an institution that transforms itself and is stable at the same time is almost never taken on. It's a paradox.

That's what you meant, I suppose, when you wrote in the same article that saving the institution is now often seen as the ultima ratio. An institution's goal is most often just preservation and survival, given the austerity times we live in.

It's true. Two years ago, Impulse was a festival that was always on the verge of being closed down. Now, it seems, we are in a better situation, and there seems to be a good future ahead. I still have to consider, however, whether the radical ideas that I might wish to fulfill or that others wish to fulfill are the best for the festival. Does it make sense to risk a festival closing down because of this or that idea? It's not about proving one's own radicalism but resisting the excuse that everybody else would do worse, and so we should hang on forever, without changing anything. It's the same dilemma. I think there are no general answers for it. You can look at some institutions and see that they have a possibility to get at least a little more radical and to rethink, to resist the urge to be lazy and to make excuses. There are others, however, where it's clear that the institution is struggling simply to survive. But there's also a point at which you must ask, what are you surviving *for*? If you cannot answer that question, then maybe it's right to let it go. Whether an institution exists or not is not the question. Merely hoping that in ten years the situation might be different doesn't function. You can also see that in moments of extreme crisis, as in Greece or the struggling Teatro Valle in Rome, very interesting things can begin to happen. But these moments last only a short time. Teatro Valle seems to be lost. There are theaters in Greece where very exciting things are happening, but we will see what happens to them in two years. Either they close and lose the fight, or they stay, perhaps as a new kind of establishment that one day just gets as boring.

Those institutional questions are never the most interesting, and yet they obsess us because they concern what we do every day.

I think those questions get interesting when we look at concrete institutions. I'm not a theorist of institutional critique, but I see in these concrete examples a lot of potential that's not used by all of us.

Traditionally, in visual arts, the curator's function involves a certain amount of institutional critique. Could theater makers take that on in a way that would be healthy and vital for the theater?

I'm still puzzled as to why institutional critique has never played a role in theater. When I try to think of examples of what one could consider as works of institutional critique in the performing arts, there are not very many. There are some works of conceptual dance that we could read as a critique of the institution of ballet—but not as critiques of concrete institutions. Perhaps Jerome Bel's *Véronique Doisneau* could be seen as a challenge to the new Paris Opera. There are very few performances, however, that deal with the conditions the performing arts are embedded within.

Is this because in the performing arts there is a different economic relationship between artist and host institution—more precarious?

Institutional critique in visual arts has almost always occurred within the institution, from artists invited in by the curators. In most of the famous examples, the critique was not happening outside of the institution. There are many reasons that institutional critique doesn't happen with the theater, but still, I am not completely satisfied with any of them. Perhaps the rise of works or group structures that call themselves institutions is a moment of institutional critique. In a way, *Die Aufführung* by Herbordt/Mohren is, if not an institutional critique, at least an institutional analysis, implicitly. It's starting, here and there.

I'm curious about your own evolution from dramaturgy and criticism into programming and curation. You started by training as a dramaturg, in the traditional sense?

Perhaps I started even earlier, because I come from a theater family. My father was a director, and my mother is an actress. One of my uncles was an actor. That I would do something that has to do with theater was probably visible rather early on, from the outset. Then, going to the University of Giessen [Institute for Applied Theater Studies, Justus Liebig University Giessen] in the mid-1990s was a major step toward programming and curation. Before I went, I thought I would be a theater director. Coming to Giessen quite quickly changed a lot of my views on theater. It made clear to me that I would not be able to do the kind of work that I was really interested in and that most of the people around me also would not be able to do it, which didn't stop them from trying. For me, however, this was immediately clear. I saw the first works of Forced Entertainment and thought, this is amazing. I would rather try to deal with this than trying anything else. It was a very fast, half-conscious decision—a recognition, maybe, rather than a decision—that I would not be a theater direc-

"Truth Is Concrete," final assembly, Steirischer Herbst, Graz, Austria, 2012. Photo: Wolfgang Silveri

tor myself. In Giessen at that time, of course, you didn't learn how to do anything. I'm exaggerating, but what Giessen offered was more a change of perspective of what theater can be.

It was a strange situation, because Giessen is in a small town where nothing happens. All you can do is hang around at the institute, because there's nothing else there. We were hanging out, all of us students up there, doing stuff but at the same time thinking, oh no, it's the wrong time, nothing is happening. We felt there were no interesting people left at Giessen anymore. Hans-Thies Lehmann was not there anymore; Andrzej Wirth was not there anymore; René Pollesch was not there any more. We felt as if we were the lost generation of Giessen.

Of course, from today's perspective, it was an incredible time. I worked and studied with the artists who formed Rimini Protokoll and She She Pop and others. From today's point of view, we were there actually at the perfect moment, but I remember sitting there thinking, what are we doing here? It was a moment where something was happening. I not only saw Forced Entertainment for the first time, but student work happening at Giessen by She She Pop. It was amazing for me to see that work then as a simple student production, which was happening for no money with five people for an audience of fifty.

For me it became clear that my work would always be related to artistic production, but I would not consider myself as an artist.

I was the dramaturg for Rimini Protokoll on the very first work that the three did together. At the same time, I began writing theater critiques for daily papers and magazines. I was a critic, and, at the same time, I was founding with friends a curators' collective called Unfriendly Takeover in Frankfurt. We called ourselves a curators' collective, but we didn't reflect very much on it. It was not as interesting for us to ask what it would mean to be a curator. We just wanted to realize projects. From today's perspective, I would say, yes, some were quite interesting.

For me it didn't make a difference that this happened all at the same time. Being a critic was becoming problematic, because, in the German tradition, you cannot be a theater critic and at the same time be involved in making theater. Of course you couldn't write about your own pieces, but you also couldn't be more generally involved. That said, [Gotthold Ephraim] Lessing liked to write about his own plays. So the German tradition is a bit complicated. Still, the reviews I would write were mainly about famous works, big shows in big city theaters. Gradually, I wrote more and more about the independent scene, but I critiqued these works maybe a little bit differently. If you're the only one coming to see a show, it's not as important to declare, "This is bullshit." Rather, I tried to explain what was happening and what was failing.

After a couple of years, I got the feeling that it's not easy to survive as a critic. I was lucky that I could write for interesting papers and make a living out of it, but it was limiting my involvement in the work itself. It became clear that I would have to decide whether I would be more involved in one or the other, because the groups that I was working with were becoming better known. It would not have been possible to stay a critic after that, I think. After I was asked to work for the festival Steirischer Herbst, I stopped writing criticism. That was the line. If you cross over and you're employed by a festival, then you cannot be a critic anymore. Since then, I still say sometimes that I am doing something like dramaturgy, dramaturgical work. I was a dramaturg for Nature Theater of Oklahoma, when we worked on *Life and Times* at Burgtheater. That was also a curatorial work, in a way, because I brought Nature Theater of Oklahoma into a very conservative theater. I would still say I do work that is closely related to artistic production, but I do not do the artistic work itself.

Why would that be curation and not dramaturgy?

For a while, at Steirischer Herbst, I liked to call myself a dramaturg, which was a contested term then. The curatorial can also mean the performative, the choreographic, and the dramaturgic. Large parts of what's described as curatorial can be called by other names. If you come from dance, you call it the choreographic; if you come from theater, you call it the dramaturgic, or you call it the curatorial— a simplification, of course. I like to talk about festival dramaturgy, rather than programming. It's the same kind of work—talking about time, about relationships. I would not be opposed to saying I'm doing dramaturgical work at Impulse. If I were working only in a German-speaking context, perhaps I would call it that. But, since this discussion about what dramaturgical work consists of is largely a German discussion, it can be limiting. In a German discussion, you could say that there has been a provocation issued from Lessing

unto now, to define what the work of a dramaturg is. But I'm not sure this discussion could happen outside of Germany. Maybe I should go back. Maybe I should call it dramaturgy again.

To reclaim dramaturgy?

Beatrice von Bismarck is now on the advisory board, which could be seen as the dramaturgical board. She always liked the idea of the dramaturg. When we first met she asked me, "How can we use dramaturgy as a model for museums?" Harald Szeemann was considered, sometimes, as a theater director.

He began as a theater director and a scenographer.

How you think about your work is formatted for you in a certain way at a certain time in your career, to a significant degree. I have a close connection to choreography. I was fortunate to be very close to people in the conceptual dance movement. I always felt, however, that I looked at dance from the perspective of theater. Even when I was working more in the field or connected to choreography, my thinking would be dramaturgical. Now, when I look at work, the dramaturgical is still there. Curating sometimes is about curating a narration. When I talk about the festival in terms of how representation is shifting between the different works, I make a narration out of the curation. It helps communicate with audiences and journalists when you can create narratives and comparisons. What happens to Milo's work in comparison to Gob Squad's work? That's a dramaturgical question. That's what a dramaturg would do. I'm fine with being called a dramaturg.

The distinctions are academic, but everyone is invested in them for material reasons. Because of the antitheatrical prejudice, theater practitioners are looking to other discourses for terminology, as if we're ashamed—we think we're the most back-ward of the arts and we need to borrow words from dance or from visual arts.

In terms of hipness, theater has been in a defensive position over the years. Now, you are beginning to see an interest in performance again. Visual art has always been the big devourer of everything—first choreography and now theater.

Visual arts institutions don't like the word theater. *They prefer* performance. *They don't want anything to do with drama or theater.*

I think theater will come eventually. I've started to hear the word *theater*, here and there. We will see; maybe it's the next thing. Of course, the discourse was first in terms of performance. This has very clearly to do with the market. The discourse in visual arts wasn't always like this. I think the discourse around theater was much richer in the 1920s. One can argue that there was at least an equal level of theatrical discourse alongside the visual arts, during the time of Bertolt Brecht and Walter Benjamin. In the nineteenth century, there was perhaps an even more interesting discourse around theater than the visual arts. And now, that might change again. It also has to do with money. As work in visual arts became less material, the market needed something else to create value around. I think that's why the term *curator* arose. As a curator, I'm not in it for the prestige. I find it rather problematic that it looks like I have prestige, that curators use the term because it's sexier. Perhaps if there were a different term, it wouldn't create this perception. Maybe the discussion around curation is a challenge for us to use the word differently or maybe to come up with something new.

To come up with another word—perhaps, to reclaim dramaturgy?

But then the word *drama* is in there, and that's also problematic.

When you think of a better word, you can originate it.

I'll start a competition—$500,000 for the person who comes up with the next word. The prize must be huge—so much money that basically everyone in the world, whether they have ever been to theater or not, wants to take part in the competition.

Every branding consultant, everyone! It seems like your interests as a curator became more political over the course of your career. There were always political dimensions to some of your research interests and your work with Rimini Protokoll and the Nature Theater of Oklahoma. Their work has strong documentary impulses and, within that, a political point of view. "Truth Is Concrete," however, was a major political effort. You conceived it before the Occupy Wall Street movement began, but it reflected that moment in every way, as it reflected Taksim Square and Tahrir Square and many other revolutionary movements. Was there a shift in your research interests as a result of the events of 2008?

Art and politics were always my interests. There was a moment in life where I considered becoming a political journalist. I was never an activist, but I was always politically engaged. In the 1980s in Germany, you could not, as a thinking person, be somehow disengaged from political movements.

However, I'm very much a part of the time I live in. I became interested in this idea of the shift, articulated by Hans-Thies Lehmann and Jacques Rancière, away from the purely aesthetic or the purely political toward the aesthetical-political. I moved in this direction with a lot of the groups and people that I mentioned. I, as did many artists in those years, felt more and more that our work was not enough, in a way. The revolutions in Egypt and Tunisia, and Occupy Wall Street, and so on, channeled a lot of this energy and shifted our interests. In the initial discussions that led to "Truth Is Concrete," we suddenly felt that it would be much more interesting for the artists to talk about these political movements, rather than what production they could do next year when they got a little bit of money. I did not suddenly become interested in politics, but rather I became interested in another kind of politics—a *Realpolitik*, to use the German term, not merely a philosophical notion of the political. That's something I believe I share with a lot of artists, a lot of thinkers, and a lot of activists, obviously.

It happened very organically. We realized the liberating potential of shifting our discourses. Coming from being an arrogant ex-Giessen student, one has a very limited and very precise view of what constitutes good art, of what art can be, and of the kind of discourse that has to be followed within an artistic work. One works from this idea, great artists emerge, and one follows their path and works with them, and so on. Eventually, a question comes up: do you renegotiate these discoveries? Do you take the time to ask, is the career that I built up ten years ago or longer still interesting? Suddenly, a different reason starts to motivate things. For "Truth Is Concrete," we invited a lot of work that two years ago I would have said was interesting but not good theater or not good art. But the criteria for judgment shifted. Instead, I wanted to see what different attempts were there to grasp reality or to influence reality or even try to change reality. When your frame of judgment shifts, you come to work with completely different people, and some of the people you've always worked with are suddenly not a part of this anymore. I learned to understand that this renegotiating of criteria and discourses is liberating.

I talked yesterday with a political theorist visiting the festival with his students from the academy. He and his students said that by being in the festival and seeing all these works you understand that the experience is less about seeing one piece and deciding whether it's good or bad. Instead, you see the next show and the next show, and you try to understand, what is each of them doing? That's not to take importance from the artwork—someone might argue that response is relativizing—but I think it rightly removes the emphasis on whether or not something works well or whether it was to your taste. Instead, the viewer asks, what is the work of Gintersdorfer/Klaßen in comparison to Gob Squad? How do these artists work? You create a different dialogue. If you curate in this mode, you can also include more work, because curation becomes less about judging quality. "Truth Is Concrete" was, of course, extreme. We had hundreds of events. When you have hundreds of events, then, you can say yes to anything. You may see something first and decide, I don't care about this. Then, you'll see the next event, and whether or not you care about an individual piece becomes less important. Maybe you'll see something you find incredibly compelling, something you would never have looked at because you had decided beforehand that the theatrical means it uses are not interesting anymore.

For me this relates to the question of how a curator can bring different people into audiences and onstage. An argument you often hear in Germany against theater that has nonwhite, non-middle-class people onstage dismisses it in terms of quality. But how can that be—that only white, middle-class people can make good theater? That cannot be. If that's the case, what kind of theater do we mean? If it means we need to question what we mean by theater, you have to take on that challenge. We needed to program

"Appropriations:
A Performative
Conference,"
Ethnologisches
Museum, Berlin,
2014. Photo:
Sebastian Bolesch

Silent University, even if it's not clear why this work would be in a theater festival, because we needed to challenge these discourses. That's what Gorki Theater in Berlin is doing from an artistic standpoint. You could say that their work is not all very good, but that simply means that they program from an artistic criteria that you would not have.

Do you mean "good" as defined by white critics?

Actually critics are very happy with the work of the Gorki Theater, because they get to meet different people there. In that example, the theater becomes the work, in a way—as a curatorial field.

What was the experience of the one-week marathon that was "Truth Is Concrete" on a personal level? How do you measure the success of an experiment like that? You've published a book, but do you also count the number of continuing collaborations that formed there as measure of your success? Or do you look at the political effectiveness of some of these projects in their home countries or these artists' influence?

I'm not very good at measuring success. Always, after everything I do, I think of what I could have done. I'm more interested in what didn't work and in what should've been done than what succeeded. The event itself was the culmination of two years of work, but even after that work is over, you still need to make sure that everything is running. I was not the best audience for "Truth Is Concrete," because I still had to be in charge, somehow. As curators, we thought about the viewer's organizational, dramaturgical, and curatorial experience. We had to ask, how do people arrive, if people are coming from all over the world? What are the rules of the game? What food do you need? How do you create an open situation within the content of the program and our aesthetic choices, while also keeping the festival open to a local audience, so that they don't feel excluded? How do you deal with days and nights? What do you need to facilitate that? What happens? How transparent is the curation? Do you invite a bunch of artists and admit to them, I used to find everything you do *wrong*? How do you deal with sponsors? How transparent are you about sponsorship? What do you pay people? What fees do you pay to whom? What exceptions do you make? Do you make exceptions? We thought so much about these details. That's what I mean when I say that performance curation is an attempt to be in control of everything, in the context of an event that is clearly something you cannot control.

The structure of the program for "Truth Is Concrete" was very rigid. We made it clear that if we said something started at twelve o'clock, then at twelve o'clock it had to start. We created a very vertical curatorial structure for the program that could operate like a machine. At the same time, we tried to think of what horizontal structures were needed. We needed a lot of space where unplanned things could happen. We thought a lot about frustration. I think frustration can be interesting, but it's hard to handle. Frustration is inevitable, because you will always miss things. A discussion finally gets interesting and you have to cut it short, so that the next thing can start. How do you make this frustration productive? You create spaces for it. We were both rigid and open. We would say, if this discussion interests you, we have another room where you can continue it for ten hours if you want—but here, now, it's over.

We adhered to an idea of an open marathon, where things could pop up and be announced spontaneously, but we didn't plan anything like that beforehand. Simply to anticipate the need was important. I remember, very vividly, that after a couple of hours into "Truth Is Concrete" it was clear that it would work. Even though there were 165 hours to go, I was not worried anymore. It was clear that either this will work, or the people who came will make it work, because they want it to work. Of course, there was a crisis in the middle of the week. I've always said, in the middle of the week, there will be a crisis, so let's facilitate it. Let's deal with it, and let's be very transparent about it.

It was also interesting for me to see people that are very critical of any hierarchical situations within a very strict curatorial structure. That's what makes the structure and the crises within it transparent. I don't like to pretend to anyone, especially within the field of politics, that I can create a very open situation that will facilitate all your needs. And yet, at the same time, that's not untrue. I did try to create the most open situation I could, where everything could happen. Yet, at the same time, there was no doubt that my cocurators and I made all the decisions, and that we were the ones who said when something ended at twelve o'clock. It was a very clear hierarchy, one you could also attack and criticize. I like to play with the two opposites—a clear curatorial statement alongside as open a space as possible. The feeling of success, for me, came not in seeing how this structure functioned but in enabling discussions and seeing frustration arise when they could not continue. People outside of each space would not discuss the weather but would continue whatever conversation they had inside. It was a relief to see that.

If "Truth Is Concrete" was a success, it's not a measurable success, because it's not mine alone. Of course, the experience rewarded me with many collaborations, friendships, working connections, and ideas, which are still vivid in what I'm doing now. I enlarged my scope of knowledge. Still, I only feel successful when I meet people who tell me that they are collaborating with someone they met at "Truth Is Concrete." I do think it made people connect and develop other projects. It was a moment in time when that was possible. We were lucky. I don't know if two years later the same thing could be done, given the political situations in all our countries. Occupy was over by then; the park had been cleared. It was a moment in time where we really felt the perspectives of the artist, the activist, and the theorist were needed.

Was it useful for you also as a blueprint for things you might like to do in the future?

It is a blueprint. Over the whole project, I learned an unbelievable amount about politics, but also about how to create an event like that, if one has the opportunity. Of course, it's not a good idea to decide to create a radical curatorial project and then afterward to find a topic for it. The idea of an exhausting marathon came out of the political experience of the time. We felt that the marathon was the right form for our ideas. I would not be interested, necessarily, in ever doing a long marathon again. It would be more interesting to do something that lasts a minute. It did teach me a quadratic approach, a calculation in terms of amount of people, in terms of dramaturgy, and in terms of time, and through this approach a lot of forms became clear for other events and other projects.

What are you working on, and what would you like to do that you haven't had a chance to do? Are you dreaming of something in particular?

In 2015, in addition to programming the Impulse Theater Festival, which is already a full-time job, I produced two big curatorial projects with Artist Organisations International, a performative conference I initiated with Jonas Staal and Joanna Warsza. Between those and the festival, I curated three big events in one year while publishing a book. I now need a moment to think and to reconsider what I would like to do next. Impulse will return next year. I am talking with Jonas Staal about how the two projects that we created with Artist Organisations International could continue, and how we could expand the idea of working with organizations of artists that each have a clear political agenda. We are talking about what that would look like—it would likely take a different form, and we would build from what we learned out of this experiment.

I also created a performative conference in an ethnological museum in Berlin ["Appropriations: A Performative Conference," Dahlem Museums, November 16, 2014], which examined the idea of performing in a museum in general and in an ethnological museum in particular. An ethnological museum is, of course, a politically charged space, and rightfully so. I was interested in the idea of a conference that purely consists of performances or performative situations, of art and not lectures. I understood lecture-performances, but what would it mean to say that a series of performances was a conference? Was it a conference?

During the event, we had groups of people moving on different paths through the museum and dealing with the space. It created some great works by Ant Hampton and Britt Hatzius, Alexandra Pirici, and Yael Bartana, among others. The conference had great results, but I believe the idea still has potential. I can't compare it easily to other projects or other artists' work, so I believe it's something that still needs to be developed. After it was over, we wondered what would happen if this conference were to become repertoire? Usually I'm not interested in repertoire, but I'm interested in the idea of repeating a conference a couple of times, without changing anything. In repertory, performances change each time, but these changes are not toward finding the next or another performance. You simply do it the same way again, in the same space, with the same artists. What would it be like to do this with a normal conference? What would it be like if you were to repeat the conference, the same way, a week later? Or a month later?

In *Second Worlds*, the 2011 iteration of Steirischer Herbst, with Gerhild Steinbuch and Hannah Hurtzig, among others, we began to ask the question of how theoretical performances and real performances can fit together. It's something I've been working on now for ten years, which I believe has culminated in this conference idea. Could this idea work within a festival? Why do a conference in a festival? Why present theory in a festival, if it's just something that a university could do better than you? Why do it? What is a conference, in terms of content but also in terms of the form? Is it something that we can contribute to, as people working in the theater?

The idea for a conference comes out of the idea of the performance-lecture. I remember very well the interest around Xavier Le Roy's *Product of Circumstances*, which was not the first lecture performance in the field of art, but within the field of dance and theater it was perceived as something completely new. Ten years ago, with the curatorial collective Unfriendly Takeover, we presented a series of lecture performances. The lecture is at the base of the idea for this conference, which hopes to push it to another level.

This work converges with a current tendency in some visual arts organizations—the public programs department also acts as a research unit, a place where performance, in particular, has found a home. Public programming becomes an institutional mechanism for working with performance.

A lot comes into my thinking from other fields, of course. This idea is not a new invention but puts things together from disparate departments. You could say that curator Hans-Ulrich Obrist had an interest in conferences. He might already have mentioned that conferences are a time-based event and with certain dynamics inherent to them. Obrist was focusing on certain aspects of the conference, like the coffee break.

Over the day in the ethnological museum, we asked that audiences commit their time, again. People wanted to know what time they could see Alexandra Pirici's piece and where. I wouldn't tell them. You have to come and commit eight hours, as people at conferences do, if they take it seriously. Perhaps not in the arts, but at an academic conference you come in the morning and stay till the night and listen to lectures. What does this do to you? You struggle against exhaustion all day. When you ask an audience to listen to ten lectures in an academic conference, or even only five, no one can tell me that not half of everyone falls asleep once in a while or thinks of something else. Why ignore this? Why not say, instead, what do we need to confront this exhaustion? Is it interesting when people get tired? When do you need food? What do you do, then, in a museum where food is not allowed? Visual artists have done work like this before in other years, but bringing it together and looking at what theater's part is in this work is still a field where more can happen.

NOTE

1. Florian Malzacher, "Empty Stages, Crowded Flats: Performative Curating Performing Arts," in *Performing Arts and the Young* (Oslo: Vidarforlaget AS, 2014), 116–27.

Section of Countries and Regions: Norway, Prague Quadrennial, Prague, 2015.
Photo: Ludek Zeuzil

Spectacular Rhizomes

Sodja Lotker

Interviewed by Tom Sellar

During her tenure as artistic director (2008–2015), scholar, curator, and dramaturg Sodja Lotker transformed the venerable Prague Quadrennial. Once an exhibition of theater design organized by national pavilions, the Quadrennial expanded with Lotker's vision to include site-specific performances, urban interventions, and original platforms for invited artists, expanding the understanding of theater design beyond traditional theater stages.

 The following conversation was recorded in New Haven, Connecticut, in November 2014, one year before her final Prague Quadrennial in 2015, when Lotker spoke at Yale University about her work on the event. It has been edited for concision and clarity. –TS

TOM SELLAR *Could you describe the evolution of the Prague Quadrennial under your leadership? What changes did you make to the format, and what themes did you engage? Were these changes to reflect a shift in world theater culture away from drama to performance?*

SODJA LOTKER I don't worry about the terminology anymore. At one point we at the Prague Quadrennial were obsessed with performance and showing that theater is a much wider discipline. But now I'm going back to the word *theater*, and I just include everything, including performance art. It's live performance. It's theater. It's dramaturgy.

 The 2015 Prague Quadrennial took place between June 18 and 28 in more than sixty indoor and outdoor venues in the center of Prague. It included more than six hundred live events and more than one hundred and fifty expositions during the course of eleven days, and it presented scenography, costume, sound, and lighting design from seventy-eight countries. The Prague Quadrennial hosted more than one hundred and eighty thousand visitors and more than six thousand accredited professionals, and more than thirteen hundred students from all over the world took part in workshops and performances.

 I use the words *scenography* and *performance design* to talk about the same thing. *Scenography* is an old word for a simple thing—stage design—that we use in Eastern Europe and Germany. Then it became a chichi word. Especially in Great Britain, they started using *scenography* to mean complexity, or the visual spatial design of a performance, a somehow holistic approach to stage design. We started using *scenography* in English because we didn't know these things. So much for precise terminology.

 The Quadrennial is a large exhibition of scenography. A group of Czech designers

Theater 47:1 DOI 10.1215/01610775-3710532

Vestyl's *Reticular Momentum* in The Tribes, Prague Quadrennial, Prague, 2015. Photo: Daniel Suska

started it in 1967. In the 1960s, theater was a good art in Eastern Europe, because communism was much more open at that point. This group of designers won a series of awards at the São Paulo Biennale in Brazil, which is a visual arts event. It was crucial that somebody from the theater won these awards at a visual arts biennale. They won a few times in a row, and then they decided to make their own event in Prague. So, this already points to the fact that scenography is interdisciplinary: it does not belong only to opera, drama, and ballet—the traditional genres.

The Quadrennial is about twelve thousand square meters of exhibition space, and it's divided by country. Like the Venice Biennale, each country has its own pavilion—a little "stage." This time [in 2015] I believe we will have over sixty countries exhibiting. We have a professional section and student exhibitions, both divided by country. We have over a thousand students come for workshops, shows,

performances, and so on. I have also curated a series of lectures, talks, discussions, and some exhibitions. It's a large event.

But to exhibit scenography is a problematic idea. Even if you manage to put the entire scenography into the exhibition space, which would be too big for most of the spaces, you would still take it out of context of the original performance. It's just a part in a totality of an art piece. I always thought it was a big problem for us, because people usually exhibit models or drawings, which is basically a documentation of the process. Some designers are really opposed to that. I was at a discussion where Finnish and Irish designers went berserk. They said, "This is ridiculous! We are not going to show our dirty laundry! You can't tell anything by this!" But theorists really like models; practitioners, not so much. The other way to exhibit scenography is by showing photos or videos—documentation of the product. But that is also not "the thing" itself.

We also give awards for stage design based on these photos, videos, and models, which I find problematic. The division by nation, which doesn't work in theater and the arts anymore, and the awards are two highly problematic things for the Quadrennial.

Unfortunately, there are not many curators of scenography. We've existed since 1967. The people who curate these exhibitions are mainly teachers or designers. Only very few of them work as curators professionally. So in the last ten to fifteen years, we did a series of symposia, educational projects, and so on to strengthen the curatorial-dramaturgical thinking of designers.

The problem with designers—at least, it used to be a problem, but it's changing drastically now—was that somehow they learned to be of service to the play or to the director. They would think of themselves as secondary within the theater team. I think the new generations are very different, but when I started that was the situation. So when designers would curate, they wouldn't be used to pushing the project or coming up with the idea. An important thing that we've been working on in the last fifteen years is to emancipate design-

ers, making room for their own projects.

In 2008, we changed the title of the Quadrennial from the Prague Quadrennial International Exhibition of Scenography and Theater Architecture—it's such a long title—to the Prague Quadrennial of Design, Performance, and Space. One thing that we wanted to lose was the word *exhibition*, because it stopped being just an exhibition. To show performance, you have to show it in the context of a live event, so it's become much more about performing, workshops, discussions, and so on. It's always been an important meeting place, too. It was always more about process and meeting rather than presenting a finished product. That's a big difference between all these posh biennales in the visual arts [and the Prague Quadrennial]. Everyone is talking to everyone. Everyone is going to everyone's workshops. Grown-ups are going to student workshops. Everybody's together. There's this really collaborative spirit in the theater, and authorship is perceived differently than in the visual arts.

We also wanted to change the words *scenography*, *stage design*. We wanted to lose the words *stage design*, *set design*, and *scenogra-*

Student Section: Serbia, Prague Quadrennial, Prague, 2015. Photo courtesy of the Prague Quadrennial

"Intersection:
Intimacy and
Spectacle," Prague
Quadrennial,
Prague, 2011. Photo
courtesy of
Prague Quadrennial

phy, and go with *performance design* and *space*. To a large extent, this move was influenced by performance studies, but with the idea to expand the understanding of what scenography is. We started to understand that performance is so much larger than theater, and we wanted to show that designers do not design only for the stage but also for fashion shows, events, installations, interventions, concerts, and so on.

For the Quadrennial and for me, it was important to say, "Theater has changed." It has changed crucially. The main change for theater is that it is leaving the building—very much so. Partially it is because we don't need cables anymore. We can be anywhere. Theater also is in search of new audiences. When I do things outside of the theater stage, I want to be with real people. I don't want people who come to the National Theatre once or twice a month. It's not an interesting meeting for me.

Boris Groys wrote in *e-flux* about the social importance of art and how visual artists are taking on this social role, because the social state has failed us. At least in Europe, it failed a long time ago. That's an interesting thought for me, because I do a lot of socially engaged theater, things in public space and so on, and people tend to say it is because there's

funding for that kind of thing. I think there is funding for that, and part of the reason that projects happen is because there is funding. Art and theater are changing. They are taking on these other roles, and it's going to change crucially in the decades to come. This social aspect is really important to the concept of the next Quadrennial.

For the 2011 Quadrennial, I curated a project called "Intersection: Intimacy and Spectacle," which was built by Oren Sagiv, an Israeli architect. In a semi-public square, we made this village of thirty boxes. I call them "white cubes, black boxes," and the idea was a joke—to try to make these ideal theaters and these ideal galleries. The biggest box was five meters by five meters, and there were some boxes that were two meters by two meters. They're really small spaces.

I wanted to create a situation where you as an audience member can walk in by yourself and enter the stage. The way it worked was that with one ticket you could come back again and again over the course of ten or eleven days, because it was impossible to go through all the boxes in one day. There's one entrance and one exit, and it was a bit of a maze. There were these clusters, so you would get lost a little bit.

I didn't label the boxes on purpose, so that you would have no clue what you're walking into. There was a map that you could use. I didn't label them, because the experience was to be the main thing. Czech theater critics, who are very conservative, had serious problems with that.

Because I had artists there such as Societas Raffaello Sanzio director Romeo Castellucci, Josef Nadj, and so on, audiences would run in! They had ten minutes or so and wanted to know, "Where is it?" They would get lost and they couldn't find it. One of them accused me of killing theater by not labeling the boxes. What was happening inside was

Section of Countries and Regions: Germany, Prague Quadrennial, Prague, 2015. Photo: Adela Vosickova

usually some kind of live performance. João Galante and Ana Borralho from Brazil had these little amplifiers inside their box, and you had to come close to hear their inner monologues. You had to really lie down with them. Brett Bailey, a South African artist, made a beautiful tiny maze. You had to go through the whole space by touching the wall, because it was completely dark.

For me it was important to show the widest variety of design and performance in all different disciplines and to make something rhizomatic—something confusing and without a center or structure or with a very vague structure. I used to call it "cultivated chaos," which I think is actually important for dramaturgy. It also was important to show that you can't define theater anymore. It's so many things. I wanted everybody to come out, to start walking down the street and say, "Ah, this is also fun! And she was miss-ing this! And she should have done this, and this should have been in the box, and that should have been in the box!" So I was trying to create something very decentralized in that sense. That was crucial for the Quadrennial, because at that point we were trying to say, okay, theater is not just models. It's not just a stage. Let's open up to all these other things.

The title of the 2015 Quadrennial is "Shared Space: Music, Weather, and Politics." The term *shared space* is used by Erika Fischer-Lichte and also by Hans-Thies Lehmann in his book *Postdramatic Theatre*. What's important for me is the social aspect of theater—that people come into the theater and they relate to each other. They are together, and they are creating certain hierarchies, relationships, and so on. What we're exploring now is how scenography and dramaturgy work in the contemporary theater, where the audience is very often not looking at a stage but

Section of Countries and Regions: Mongolia, Prague Quadrennial, Prague, 2015.
Photo: Martina Novozamska

instead joins in the playing space. Somehow in that sense, the design is not only a dramaturgical aspect of the performance, where the characters and the performers get into certain spatial relationships or visual relationships, but also a social aspect, because you have a live audience that comes into these relationships. How these hierarchies and positionings are created is one of the important things.

Can you say more about the difference between dramaturgy and curation in terms of identifying potentiality?

In the theater, when you work with community or work site specifically you start with something authentic, a material. It's documentary theater in a way. You have to start reading from the material; you're not reading from your head. You're not writing something

that comes from you, you're reacting to the thing. The way I work with my students is like the Chinese *I Ching* (Book of Changes). You have something and you read what it's telling you so that you become a reflection of the thing. It's not a rational construction. It's a reaction to the thing, and it's still you. But for me it's not a question that you have already answered.

I think this reading from the material and the idea of potential are crucial for dramaturgy and curating. Curators should never make something out of nothing. If you want to change something, you have to scan and see where the potential of the situation is and then let it grow. If you start from nothing, then it's not going to grow. People who are talented enough to do that should try and work with that as much as possible.

When I started working on the theme for the 2015 Quadrennial—music, weather, and politics—I realized that I was looking for scenography as a power that is beyond visual, that is actually a dramaturgical power. Something in flux, something that has—like music, weather, and politics—incredible power over our lives. I wanted to point to the idea that scenography is becoming more like dramaturgy rather than something visible. Something that determines these relationships, a journey, a meeting of bodies and minds, or hierarchies, and so on, in space.

I was worried when I started talking about this to designers, but it was incredible how much even the older designers were really into it, and how they completely knew exactly what I was talking about. Moving away from design as visual, the way I think about it now is that scenography is what I call a performative environment. It's a very complex thing that is visual, spatial, and has its own character. It's like a living thing rather than something static. This idea is very important not only for how we make design, which obviously we do, but also for how design makes us. Where is the authorship and control? How does that relationship work?

Scenography as politics will be important in the 2015 Quadrennial. Henri Lefebvre, the social geographer, said that in addition to what he calls architectural space (physical space) and socially constructed space, there's also practice space. This practice space changes the architectural and socially constructed space. This idea of change and that you change something by practice is very, very crucial to my thinking about the Quadrennial. I think that change is very necessary in society today. That's why I was talking about artists doing all the social projects and so on.

A few years ago in Estonia, I met Vallejo Gantner, the artistic director of PS122 [at the time]. He was talking to me about Occupy Wall Street with great passion. He was saying that they use masks and are building all these scenographies. They have this tent, and art is really alive there. Theater is necessary. Then he stopped and said, "But none of the professional theater people are there. When I realized that, I thought to myself, if we are not there, where are we?" I still get goosebumps to this day thinking about that. When he said that, I almost started crying and said, "Oh god, what are we doing?" He said, "I was sitting in my office at PS122, and it was completely empty. I was excited about them doing theater, and I realized that we really have to change our way of thinking. If we want to have some meaning, we have to move." Obviously, moving into the streets and outside of the stage is a way to do it, but it's not the only way. I think it's a first step to go into the city again with people, but I think it also should and could happen onstage.

Is cultivated chaos a political idea as well as an aesthetic one?

It's mainly aesthetic, but obviously it's political. And it's psychological, too. I actually like being in that situation where I don't completely know exactly what's going to happen. That's what theater is: entering relationships with other people in which you are not sure what's going to happen.

The national exhibition proposals in 2015 seem to be responding very well to the new ideas of scenography, and the majority of exhibitions are becoming relational scenographies, where designs come through the presence of audiences, and that presence somehow finishes the design. So most of the exhibitions are going to be kind of installations in themselves, little "stages" where you enter a set of relationships. This is "soft" politics, the sociopolitics of theater.

Discussion at the Colloredo Mansfeld Palace, Prague Quadrennial, Prague, 2015. Photo: Adela Vosickova

Can I ask you to back up a little bit to tell us a bit about the mechanics of this, starting with your curatorial prompt—music, weather, and politics—and the process that follows?

It's quite complicated. I'm the artistic director of the Quadrennial, not the curator. There are at least another eighty to one hundred curators working under me, because each country is curating and organizing itself. And the way it works is that I propose a concept and I inspire them. For the symposium this year, we also met everyone in Prague, got together to talk about the concept, and then [the curators] go on and do what they need to do. I have no veto, but I can guide them. Basically I am dra-

maturging more than curating in the picking and deciding.

Usually a huge organization or a ministry of culture appoints a curator for the national pavilion and provides money, so it's really diplomatic. That's the big part of the international and student exhibition. We also do smaller projects—smaller than twelve thousand square meters—that are partially through open call. The artists submit and we choose. I curate some of the projects; I also curate workshops for students and discussions and so on. In addition to the national curators, I also have six other main curators. It's very much about curating some pieces but also overseeing the totality. You can understand why I talk about cultivated chaos—I really cannot influence what somebody from Macau does. I don't know where they're coming from, so how would I decide whether or not they're doing something good or bad? Maybe in their context it's important. Also, my point of view is European, so it can be tricky territory. I have to decide how to help those that are coming from completely different contexts, and context is obviously a crucial idea for dramaturgy and curating. With the national curators, that's what we were working with. We're trying to teach them what curatorship is, to understand you're coming from Macau, you're exhibiting in Prague, the audience is diverse and from all over the world, and they come from completely different theater cultures. You have to create something that is really experiential or you have to explain it well, but you can't over explain it either. Cultural context is highly problematic.

I think relational space is also a very important curatorial and dramaturgical idea—the idea that you're situating and placing. That's what you do as a curator, you're placing something. You're contextualizing it by placing it in a certain place. When we learn about dramaturgy in school, we're taught that the situation—the character—is the most important thing. I'm going back to this idea of dramatic situation, and I think of the exhibition as a situation, as a station. That's why I'm talking about performative environments, because that's a dramatic situation, in a way. That's what I try to do as a curator. I try to create open situations for people to relate in some way. It's like a set of rules but open to interpretation. That's my expanded idea of situation.

Another interesting thing that I'm seeing in the proposals from the national exhibitions are the descriptions of scenography. It's described as site, space, place, room, station, shaky ground, territory, base location, and landscape; more abstractly, it's described as locality, atmosphere, a way to do something, spatial practice in collectively determined space, modified map, in-between place, space's potential stage, something placed and displaced, imagined space, ritualized space, scenographers' dreams, idealized space, and so on. What's interesting for me here is that the designers themselves have stopped perceiving design as something static. It's something that's performing, something that does—scenography as a road rather than a place.

What's really important is something that I think of as third space. We all know that theater at its core is bodies of actors, props, chairs, objects. But there's also the whole imagination of all the artists and all the audience and all that happens in people's heads rather than onstage. That's really beautiful. When he retells Lefebvre, Edward Soja, the social geographer, talks about the "third space": the space where imagination and reality are not divided. There's a great potential in the theater in that sense.

Reclaiming imagination is really important to me now. We did a symposium in 2013 called "Layering Reality: The Right to Mask" over two days in Prague, and everyone was masked. I was very proud of it. We were exploring mask on the verge of theater and the political, because wearing a mask at a demonstration is forbidden in many countries, which I find highly problematic. The symposium was lovely, because we were in the underground of the National Gallery in Prague, which is a huge modernist building. You go in and it is like a little secret society—psychiatrists, architects, anarchists, theater people, and designers—everyone masked. The moderators were masked. The first day we managed to be masked the whole day, but on the second day, it started shredding, because you couldn't hear or see. But it was fun while it lasted. For me, it's about creating a situation.

The Cloud
installation, Prague
Quadrennial,
Prague, 2015. Photo:
Katerina Krusova

I have a project called The Tribes that is partially through a call and partially curated. I was exploring different artists and the use of mask in art. I wanted to use the public space as a gallery and living people as the artifacts exhibited. It's going to be groups of masked people—full-body masks—walking around the city. There's going to be a specifically designated route that they will walk: out from the museum to the underground, take two metro stops, get off, go into a supermarket, buy chocolate, go into a park, sit at a specific bench, and it's going to be every hour—a different group of people doing exactly the same thing. Every artifact is going to be seen only by the people working in the metro, in the supermarket. A microaudience will see all the pieces. A group of photographers will follow and take photos at exactly the same place, so we're also going to make a Facebook exposition. It's going to be a micro- and macro-exposition.

It's another experiment in how to exhibit scenography. In a similar experiment in the spring of 2014, I invited four Czech designers who were between thirty and forty years old to meet and to show each other their work. Then I asked each of them to pick another artist and to make a video essay about the artist's work, to retell the work. The idea was that you're not really making a new piece of art. I called them scenography video essays, and it was very much about recycling and recontextualizing. It's very much about retelling the thing, in a way.

In one project, the designer recorded a dialogue between designer and director. She took the crucial things out and then asked people from the street to come into the studio and read the sentence of this dialogue. She had old people, young people, kids. The way it gets recontextualized when it's said without knowing what it really means is really beautiful. Again, we didn't build anything. Instead, we used all the scenography parts from the National Theater.

Can you describe some of the limitations and the challenges of what you're doing?

The problem with a Quadrennial is that it's every four years, so the process is extremely slow. I wish it were a biennial, because then the trial and error phase would be quicker-for all of us. The Quadrennial is still an event that is sponsored by the Ministry of Culture of the Czech Republic, which provides for the majority of financing.

What about the public?

The majority of our audiences are the people exhibiting. So you're visiting, exhibiting, and watching. For me, cultivating the artists is the core of the thing. I don't focus so much on wide audiences. I try to create projects that are simple and very telling. I try to make things that are conceptual yet colorful and can be enjoyed by a wide audience. I don't try to do very intellectual, fragile things, because that would disappear anyway, and the Quadrennial is somehow too big for that. We don't really cultivate our audience. We try to create these experiential and colorful spaces, and the people come and they enjoy it. It's a little bit schizophrenic, because you're making a big change for the artists and then a completely new thing for the audience. But because it's every four years, you cannot cultivate the audience; they forget by the time it happens again. That's a big problem with audiences as well as with building the organizational team of the Quadrennial, because you're starting from scratch every time. It's a big problem with sponsors. Nobody wants to sponsor something that happens every four years and then everybody forgets about it. The timing is a little bit "nonhuman" in a way.

You have said that you are worried about the theatrical imagination and therefore the social imagination being diminished. There's a shift to the sociological that has held back other aspects of performance and theater. Has the search for authenticity—to connect with real spaces, real people, real communities—limited the power to imagine through fiction and through scenography? How do you arbitrate between those two desires?

I don't know. I'm not really sure how to answer your question. That's a great paradox, but I'm now in between the thinking, so I have not decided. I work with Lotte van den Berg, a Dutch director. We do this proj-

Section of Countries and Regions: Brazil, Prague Quadrennial, Prague, 2015. Photo courtesy of Prague Quadrennial

Section of Countries and Regions: Hungary, Prague Quadrennial, Prague, 2015. Photo: Martina Novozamska

ect called Cinéma Imaginaire, where the performer gives a set of instructions to the audience on how to watch. They are in a public space and they are shooting their own movie, just by watching. You're following instructions, and you're shooting a movie. It takes about two hours, you're using different tools to shoot a movie, and then in the end, we meet in a theater, everybody sits onstage, and everybody tells a little moment and they become the performance. Lotte and I talk a lot about this third space, and that's also what Benjamin Verdonck, a Belgian artist, talks about. It doesn't matter if it's authentic or colorful. I think this connection of real and imaginary is where I find the inspiration for the potential change.

So the audience in that situation is authentic. They're a community. In a sense,

we are working in the community. But they're using their imaginations, so it doesn't have to be literally theatrical. The dramaturgical framing is theatrical anyway. In one talk, I said that theater is always third space. And then Lotte came to me and said, "But you're wrong. Theater is a third space when we *make* it a third space." That was a really nice realization for me. Because somehow I thought, well, you're going to the theater, and it's—no, it's because somebody still decides. Somebody gives these other people a possibility.

To what extent do you think about engaging urbanist questions—questions about gentrification, or private versus public space—these questions that artists are asking frequently?

It's definitely a hot topic nowadays. Within the Quadrennial we have a big architecture section, theater architecture. The whole exhibition this time will be dedicated to the city as theatrical space and the theatricality of the city. So individual countries are working with that, with urbanism, and so on. When I work as a dramaturg, I do a lot of public space site-specific work and all those urban journeys of different kinds—media or new media, sound, and so on. But the things that I curate for the Quadrennial—I purposely don't think about "healing" the city, because I don't think that's our job. Our job is to change the thinking about scenography and theater, and taking the scenography outside of the theater venue is a big step. For me, the priority is what you would think of as the aesthetic part of the thing. It's more about healing scenography than about healing the city—so healing the scenography with the city. Also, the Quadrennial is really big, so you cannot do projects that are heavily researched or take on a lot of responsibility. It's more about creating presence and starting things. When I do things for the Quadrennial in public spaces, it's about creating the presence of design and making the friction—the meeting with the public space—but not taking on a social role directly. That the social aspect is always there when you create the presence, because you're creating a certain dialogue no matter how short-lived it is. I tend not to take the responsibility of healing the city, because that would be a very, very big project.

I want to ask you about which organizations or initiatives are inspirational to you. You've already mentioned Creative Time in New York and the Steirischer Herbst initiatives led by Florian Malzacher.

I also like the de Appel Gallery Amsterdam for visual arts. But I'm deeply, deeply inspired by Artangel, a London organization. They always make these projects that don't fit in any category or any traditional space. They don't

fit performance, and they seem to be undoable, but at the same time they're extremely logical. That's really important in my work. I take genres or forms of exhibition and theater performance to be social constructions, so I always question the genre itself. What I try to do is shift the genre. That's why, in The Tribes project, I take the public space as a gallery and the body as artifact. It's reframing, questioning the genre.

You've talked about wanting to "emancipate" scenography. What would happen after emancipation? What do you mean, and what kind of hopes would you attach to it?

The designer is traditionally perceived as somebody who is a service to the play, and depending on the culture, to the playwright or the director. It's somebody who fulfills somebody else's dreams, while partially fulfilling their own. But the emancipation of the scenographer is not really a revolution. It's pointing to the fact that scenographers and designers don't only do traditional projects in which they are a service group to the play. They also do their own projects: different installations, interventions, site-specific walks, VJ-ing, fashion shows, and so on. Many times the scenographer initiates the project. I think it's more about saying theater has changed, and with the theater, the scenographer has also changed. Which is also true about dramaturgy and about all the roles, especially with collective creation and devised dramaturgy and all those situations where there's no clear leader. It was really important not only to say that theater has changed but also to inspire the designers that exhibit at the Quadrennial to create the whole performative environment themselves and that they can start without these other artists.

Lars Jan's
*The Institute of Memory
(TIMe)*, REDCAT,
Los Angeles, 2016.
Photo: Lars Jan

Silos, Empathy, and Open Platforms

Miranda Wright

Interviewed by Tom Sellar

TOM SELLAR *Could you talk about your background and how you came to independent curating of contemporary performance? Do you have a theater or a dance background?*

MIRANDA WRIGHT Like many people, I became involved with theater in high school, and then went to Southern Utah University for my undergraduate degree. While there, I spent a lot of time with the Utah Shakespeare Festival's education department. After graduation I wasn't really sure what to do with myself. I had a major in theater and a minor in business management. I was then recruited by CalArts' MFA producing program. That seemed like a good move for me since I wasn't really sure how to make a career for myself in southern Utah working in theater, and I felt like I needed to balance traditional theatrical training with something that may be more exciting or on the outer edges of the form.

While studying at CalArts, I became friends with some really incredible artists. They were the first artists I worked with after graduation: Lars Jan, Chi-wang Yang and Cloud Eye Control, Miwa Matreyek, Emily Mendelsohn, and Deborah Asiimwe, an incredible and amazing playwright and arts leader from East Africa. This is the cohort of artists that I started out with, and that really happened because we all graduated around 2008 when the economy had tanked. In Los Angeles especially, there wasn't really an infrastructure to support the development of new work unless you had already reached a certain level within your career.

So my friends and I started making work. They would make work, and I'd learn on the job, in the sort of real-world conditions outside of a graduate school context. I figured out how to provide some kind of platform of support for this work to happen. So one thing led to another, and the work started traveling internationally. The first project I did out of graduate school was *The Closest Farthest Away* with Sage Lewis and Chi-wang, which performed at the Teatro Mella in Cuba, and then Miami Light Project presented it in Florida. It was sort of a huge international collaboration with artists in Los Angeles, Havana, and New York dealing with political and social issues between the US and Cuba at that time. It was a beautiful project.

At the same time that project was happening, I was working as an assistant to Joan Stein, who was Steve Martin's producing partner. She was producing both pre-Broadway shows and Showtime series. Joan

Theater 47:1   DOI 10.1215/01610775-3710544

Project Por Amor
and Sage Lewis's
*The Closest Farthest
Away*, Teatro Mella,
Havana, 2009.
Photo:
Project Por Amor

was the first person to actually fire me from a job. My attention was on this project in Cuba, and I couldn't fully support her and her productions, so she said, "Look, I think you're going to be off to a great path, but this is clearly not the right path for you." And she was right. My path is not the commercial or mainstream musical path. I am much happier working independently.

After *The Closest Farthest Away*, I worked with Deborah Asiimwe and Emily Mendelsohn on a four-year-long project called *Cooking Oil*. It was based in East Africa and we eventually brought it back to the US. It had its US premiere in 2013 in Los Angeles. That's the year my career started to take off. That fall, Radar LA came back with its second festival, and Center Theatre Group commissioned

me to produce a project called *You Should Have Stayed Home, Morons*, directed by Manuel Orjuela from Bogotá and written by Rodrigo Garcia.

That was also the year that I launched the LAX Festival at the Bootleg Theater. The Bootleg is unique in that it has one of the better stage spaces in town, but it also has a model of supporting itself through a for-profit, music-presenting model. Many bands come through the Bootleg to perform late at night. So to create a festival there I programmed theater and then the audience could walk out to live music playing every single night of the week. So I founded Los Angeles Performance Practice (LAPP) in 2010 to provide a producing infrastructure for these projects, responding mostly to the needs of my peers.

Three years later the LAX Festival was launched, because one of the things I noticed was that there just weren't enough presentation opportunities for the work that we were producing to actually happen in Los Angeles. We were producing work that would travel internationally, that would be produced by major national partners, developed through residencies out of state, but it would not actually happen in our own city. So the LAX Festival did two things. One, it provided a performance opportunity for local artists in LA, and two, it countered the programming of Radar LA and highlighted what was happening on the ground in the city. I can say this now, recognizing that I was fully naive at the time! And, I say this with all respect for the curators of Radar LA, but this was part of my intention. I realized that some of the younger artists weren't really getting a shot at visibility within this huge international platform, so we very intentionally wanted LAX alongside Radar LA to draw that attention to local emerging artists.

LA has seen a remarkable resurgence in the arts scene, fueled by these big museum projects. There's a lot of interest in West Coast artists again. The whole city is having this amazing moment, it seems, retrospectively starting around the time that you were launching these initiatives. So why is there a problem for contemporary performance makers that are based here? You said there's a lack of platforms, and yet, it seems like there's a lot of theaters, art museums, and gallery spaces. So what's the problem?

Let's play a game. How many presenters of contemporary performance in New York City can you name that support local artists? I mean, provide residency space or even just provide an opportunity to show their work.

PS122, New York Live Arts, Crossing the Line, HERE...

In LA, we have REDCAT, Highways Performance Space, and then, dot dot dot. Center Theatre Group commissions some, but it's very much along the lines of a certain scale of theater project that can happen. And then we have a number of small initiatives. And maybe that's part of what's invigorating the scene here: Machine Project and Human Resources are two smaller institutions that support visual arts and performance; Show Box LA, Meg Wolfe's contemporary dance organization, just got a space last month; and Pieter is a performance space that's really making a huge difference in supporting the contemporary dance and performance here in LA. But these places are quite small, with very limited funds to actually commission, and limited space, so when you produce publicly maybe only thirty people can actually see it at a time. That's the infrastructure problem.

Then we have this whole other slew of theaters. We probably have more physical theater spaces than New York City, and part of that is the ninety-nine-seat theater scheme, which is built on the backs of actors who have moved to LA in order to participate in the TV and film industry here. Many of those theaters have resident companies whose members pay to participate, with the intent to bring in agents who might elevate these actors' careers. And then we have this huge movement of galleries raining down onto downtown LA and the arts district. The Santa Monica Museum of Art announced last month that it is relocating from Santa Monica to a warehouse in the arts district in downtown LA and renaming themselves the ICA LA. So there is a true movement in the visual arts world toward this part of Los Angeles.

I recently worked with a performance curator at a really nice midsize art exhibition space called The Mistake Room in Los Angeles. They curated their first performance residency with Jennie Liu and Andrew Gilbert's performance/installation *House Music*. Jennie has very smartly been tracking into performance within visual art contexts. Her work is conceptually and visually strong, and she's one of the most skilled and magnetic performers I've seen. As well suited as *House Music* was for a gallery or visual art environment, we came up against some stark cultural differences in process and terminology between the performing arts and performance in art spaces.

Speaking generally, there seems to be a real gap between performance and the visual arts world in Los Angeles, even when curators are very genuinely interested in the form. Basic conditions for performance to succeed are foreign: rehearsal requirements, materiality of the form (costumes being one example of a tension-provoking material), interactions between audience and performer, and especially financial models required to support artists working in performance (compensation for time and people vs. the acquisition of objects).

I've also observed a gap in audiences for either side of this performing arts/performance art spectrum—even among artists who make up so much of our audience here. Those who come from theater have a difficult time appreciating nonlinear performance in a gallery setting, where often concept and visual composition override storytelling priorities. And, those audience members who frequently attend art openings and gallery shows react negatively to the stigma of theater. So there's a lot of work to do to bring those two worlds together.

We do see José Luis Blondet, LACMA's [Los Angeles County Museum of Art] wonderful curator for special initiatives, commissioning new performance works by local artists. He comes from the Latin American theater world, and I really think he's setting a spectacular example for the rest of the art world in what's possible for performance in our larger arts institutions. I hope the work we're doing with LAPP and the LAX Festival can help in further bridging these gaps.

Philadelphia has tremendous local support, the Pew Charitable Trusts, for example, who are interested for philanthropic or ethical reasons in funding local companies, creating sustainable structures for local ensembles, new nonprofits, or even individual artists. Is there the equivalent of such a thing in Los Angeles? Is there a network or a structure that makes that possible for these artists?

Unfortunately, no. There's a huge interest in Los Angeles in immersive theater, a decade behind New York and London. And as LA is the home of all sorts of media, a lot of studios are interested in developing content for virtual reality, and these studios are looking to invest in content that relates very directly to immersive theater. We don't have a lot of immersive theater going on in the city, so there's room for opportunity and funding.

Part of the problem is that most of the national foundations, like the New England Foundation for the Arts and Creative Capital, for example, are based on the East Coast. I ran a study to see which artists were receiving funding from these big national funders since 2010, and not surprisingly, most of the artists who are receiving funding from these national funders are East Coast, specifically New York–based artists. Philadelphia is well represented as well. The artists who receive repeat support from these funders in LA are

very specifically focused on projects that are socially driven and community based.

What I'm getting at is that when you're in New York there seems to be some support for artists who are working on social issues *and* in contemporary aesthetics, like Okwui Okpokwasili. I'm not even saying that she's well funded—I don't think that anyone right now is well funded—but there are opportunities for someone like her, working in socially and politically minded ways and *also* in new and exciting aesthetic forms to make new work. In Los Angeles, there's seemingly no acknowledgment of aesthetic or formal experimentation, but you're at an advantage if you're

working directly with community-driven social issues and creative placemaking here. The National Performance Network does a really great job with geographic diversity in their grantees, by the way. So there are, with REDCAT support, local artists who are receiving that money. But the bottom line is there just isn't enough money in the country to support all these artists, and Los Angeles—as the second largest city—has pulled an especially short straw.

In Los Angeles specifically, many of our local funds have just dried up. The Center for Cultural Innovation used to have an investing-in-artists grant, a $10,000 award,

Deborah Asiimwe's
Cooking Oil,
The National
Theatre, Kampala,
Uganda, 2010.
Photo:
Miranda Wright

that now only funds artists in the Bay Area. The Durfee Foundation used to offer the Artists' Resource for Completion grant, a smaller grant around $3,500 that would enable artists to tour their work outside of LA, but that fund also ended. When Olga Garay-English was the head of the Department of Cultural Affairs in Los Angeles she initiated several amazing platforms that made room for international collaboration and exchange with LA artists. All of those programs have been cut since her departure. The city's funding priorities are really based around creative placemaking as it relates to the mayor's Great Streets Initiative, which is a very intentional development effort by the city planning arm.

So the financial picture is pretty grim. Individual philanthropy here focuses on the larger institutions. Center Theatre Group, LA Opera, and LA Philharmonic are receiving the bulk of any individual philanthropy. One program to be highlighted is the Sherwood Award program, in honor of Richard E. Sherwood, which is managed by Center Theatre Group. The Sherwood Award is given to one theater-based artist per year, along with a $10,000 unrestricted grant. You might think that since Los Angeles is the hub of

new media that the companies and individuals working in new media and with new technologies in entertainment would be really anxious to fund the generation of artists who are working outside of the norm, and in innovative ways, but that isn't really happening. It's not a direct line of return of investment.

You mentioned that things are really shifting, because downtown is becoming a hub now for the arts. Does that make it easier for audiences because they know where to look? My experience is that Los Angeles is so unfathomably vast, and yet, if you're not from here you really don't know where to look because it's so huge. But if we are able to identify platforms downtown, does that make it easier for us to find the artists? Is there an audience that's being created because there's a centrality now that wasn't in place ten years ago?

We may be going in that direction, I hope we are, at least. As of now, audiences are still tied to specific venues. REDCAT has done a really outstanding job at generating and cultivating an audience for contemporary work. Most shows that I see at REDCAT are really fantastic. The trickier thing comes when you're an organization like mine who doesn't have a home venue, so I'm developing and cultivating an audience for every specific project that I produce. We are developing a little bit more of a track record with the LAX Festival, so that's becoming marginally easier, but it's still pretty challenging.

There is a very strong audience for theater here in Los Angeles, but they may not be an adventurous audience. But there are some adventurous audience members who are going to all of the art openings and visiting all the galleries. There's still a line down the block at the new Broad Museum. The music industry has an outstanding audience here, especially for new and experimental music. But the audiences still seem to be somewhat siloed. To get a person from the line at the Broad to come and see a piece of performance that I'm programming, I really have to program that performance in a space that is not called a theater. Because if a space is called a theater they'll be less likely to come in.

So there's going to be an emergence of new audiences, an emergence of new support systems and platforms for artists to develop work. We're on the edge of that right now, but we're not quite there. There's still an element of LA being the Wild West in terms of contemporary performance. We're still calling out high noon draws and figuring out how to make things work in sometimes brutal conditions.

So these various needs that we've just identified are the reasons for your founding Los Angeles Performance Practice (LAPP). Why do you call it that, and what are the goals of this initiative?

Well, I'm horrible at naming things, so I just put the mission into a title! First, it's important to me that it's rooted in Los Angeles and that it's serving artists within LA. Second, we have performance, because I'm primarily interested in contemporary performance. Finally, *practice* really became a key term. I didn't want to found a production company, and I didn't really want to initiate any new organizational infrastructure that would be institutionalized too quickly. The goal is to provide a platform for a practice, for an ongoing practice that can then lend toward an innovation of ideas, a way of working, or a methodology for the artists who are here. So LAPP was founded as an open platform that also happened to provide the infrastructure that producing needs, like accounting, business infrastructure, and so on.

Do you have a set number of artists that you select and advocate for as an organization? Or is it an ever-changing series of artists and priorities?

One of the goals with my own practice is to establish long-term commitments to artists. There's no set number of artists that I can work with; it's just based on my own personal capacity and the capacity of the organization. There are artists whom I'm deeply committed to, whom I have been committed to since the very beginning. The artists who come into the network come in on a project basis, so they're not on contract necessarily, but the organization is incredibly loyal. We still produce specific projects, and we then promote these projects, but the artists that I work with regularly are still Lars Jan, Jennie Liu, Zoe Aja Moore, and Janie Geiser. These four have been with me for some years now.

And there are always new artists who come in and out of the infrastructure, depending on the project. Because Los Angeles is so big and there are so many artists, I consider myself a producer who has to curate a roster of artists to work with. And part of that curation is knowing which artists I am equipped to create conditions for and care for in a way that's genuine and mutually beneficial. When

Jennie Liu / Grand Lady Dance House's *House Music*, The Mistake Room, Los Angeles, 2016. Photo: Keith Skretch

I talk to new artists I'm always feeling out if I can support them with what I have and if they'll benefit from that support. So I have to do a lot of negotiating in my own head about how I spend my time and the resources that I have access to. It is certainly a goal for the infrastructure itself to have artists I'm producing as part of Los Angeles Performance Practice to show work first at the LAX Festival and then go on to have touring and presentation opportunities both nationally and internationally. But as with any kind of relationship building, sometimes you realize it's not a good fit and you have to let that go.

So LAPP has formed various kinds of strategic alliances, one with LAX, and it's, well, a sort of affiliated and yet separate entity, because you do it with Bootleg…

Well, the Bootleg is a venue, and I rent the venue. They coproduce by providing production support, and I am fully responsible for the curation of the festival. In the coming years you'll see us moving away from the Bootleg. One of the issues with the Bootleg is that they have music programming late at night, which is sort of a blessing and a curse, but I can't program late into the evening there.

So the perception is it's still like Under the Radar at the Public Theater, where it's like this extension of the place.

Yes, that's something I sort of need to work out a little bit. But this year's festival has four different sites, so we're slowly growing and moving outside of that one-venue model to a model similar to the Fusebox Festival in Austin or the TBA Festival in Portland, where we're working with several sites across the city and slowly, organically growing the festival to be more of a citywide event.

And when will that be, out of curiosity?

2017 will be the fifth year. I'm hoping that the fifth year anniversary of the LAX Festival will take place in at least five different sites.

Spaced out throughout the year or in a specific month?

This year's festival is going to be September 22 through October 2, and we'll be at the Bootleg Theater, Automata in Chinatown, an open warehouse in the very popular arts district, and, finally, we'll be working on a site-specific project at Union Station with Metro Art Presents. We're spreading out. We're also looking to have a more structured conversation series in true LA style at a vegan juice bar and restaurant at brunchtime on the weekends.

Right now LAPP has three distinct programs. The first is still creative producing and managing projects that tour. The second program is the annual LAX Festival and other periodic presenting platforms. The third program is brand new, and it's called NEW/NET. Since my own capacity to support projects through these other two platforms is very limited, NEW/NET will be an open-source platform for artists to develop their own skills and capacities, creatively and administratively. NEW/NET now exists in two forms. The first is that I do a free advice session at the Ace Hotel on a monthly basis, and any artist can sign up for a free one-on-one consultation hour with me. The second is that in the fall we'll be launching a curated list of events that's citywide, so when people do come in from out of town they'll have some kind of source to understand what's happening. We'll establish a workshop series and conversation series along with the platform in the coming months. We're also entering into web-based publishing to develop ways of contextualizing contemporary performance in our city—for our own projects, and those presented at partnering organizations.

And you also have an alliance with UCLA?

I have a few other partnerships, one specifically with the Center for the Art of Performance (CAP) at UCLA with Kristy Edmunds. I am the curatorial artist-in-residence at CAP UCLA right now. I'm curating a series of local residencies for artists to develop work that's in the very early stages of development. Hopefully that will feed into a work-in-progress series at the LAX Festival and then ideally those projects will find some other form of support either locally or nationally for their ongoing development as we produce them fully.

How did the LAX Festival come to be?

The launch of LAX was in line with the Radar LA in 2013. I wanted to make some kind of presentation opportunity for local artists with whom I was working at the time to show work and receive some form of national visibility. The first year of the LAX Festival was designed primarily for that purpose. We knew that a lot of guests would be coming from out of town, producers, presenters, writers, and funders, so we wanted to point some arrows at the emerging artists in the city. To be honest, I also did it as a way to aggregate costs, because a lot of artists were looking for a way to self-produce and talked to me about helping them self-produce a run of their show while everyone was in town. I said, "That's crazy, let's just join forces and make a festival out of it." I didn't know if it would be an annual event, but the response was just so warm and so great, especially from the local artist community. They really appreciated another opportunity to show work and even appreciated another opportunity to see one another's work. That doesn't happen here a lot.

You set it up to be for the visitors, but actually the people who really wanted it were local.

That's right. And the people coming in from out of town seemed to have a really great response to it as well, so it served its initial purpose. And what would happen is I would be in the lobby and some artist I didn't know would come up and say, "I've been wondering where this scene was in LA, and I just found it!" So it became critically important for me to continue on this track.

We did it a second year, and the second year I was so proud of the program. The program featured out-of-town artists too, like Phil Soltanoff and Holcombe Waller, alongside local projects. But the second year was just not the same. There wasn't the same local energy built around it. There was no other large festival going on. There weren't any out-of-town presenters coming in for this festival, and audience development was really hard. I spoke to Ron Berry, who founded the Fusebox Festival, about it, and he said, "Yes, that's the second year slump. You just have to do it again." I was so devastated by the second year. I was so proud of this lineup, and I felt that I made great strides as a curator. And Ron said, "That's the second year, it's awful. Do it a third time."

We did it a third time last year, and, luckily, our single ticket sales doubled from the past year. And, we had five people who came to every single event! They were our first festival pass holders, and it felt like a big deal—like we're finally gaining traction locally. So there is now finally some momentum to keep this thing alive. But regardless, across the three years, we make space for work that's not finished yet, work in development, and we also have room for work that is ready to tour. And those simultaneous platforms have made such a difference in terms of artists developing their portfolios, having work samples to submit to some of these national funding platforms, and being able to engage

with presenters on the national level. That didn't happen before. Last year I was able to fly in some presenters from out of town, which proved to be really important. Angela Mattox came from PICA, Lane Czaplinski from On the Boards, and artists knowing that they were around was really encouraging.

So you're saying, you've made great influence, but you still have a way to go, because these aren't things you see so much in that circulation. What would it take to get them fully there, do you think?

Part of it is this residency with CAP UCLA. The studios that people are working within to make their work are so small that they're prohibiting larger ideas from coming into play. So I'll bring an artist into the Royce Hall rehearsal room, and they'll spend a full day out of a week by themselves in the middle of the space writing or walking around, and just mapping out ideas. You could look at that as a poor use of space, but I see an artist imagining a work that can actually scale to a national level as opposed to being performed in a storefront or living room. That's part of this ongoing development of infrastructure.

Jennie Liu is developing a new project with CAP UCLA, and that will then provide a platform for her for national visibility. It's putting the stepping stones in place, and we're making our way through it. But it still blows my mind that this didn't exist in Los Angeles before! I mean, why wasn't there a platform like this in Los Angeles?

Well, there are amazing precedents. The scale and ambition of the Los Angeles Festival in 1984, 1987, and 1990 now seem unimaginable to me in an American context. Some of that was due to the presence of the Olympics and the designation of funds for a cultural component, but the city was able to keep it going for a time. Are you aware of

House Music,
The Mistake
Room, 2016. Photo:
Jonathan Potter

*such precedents or predecessors in what you're
doing? How much connection do you have to this
previous generation of initiatives in LA?*

I think the critical thing is that the LAX Festival started so small—the first year my budget was $30,000 in total. That's tiny! And we're growing organically and incrementally. If you look at the Olympics Arts Festival in 1984, that grew into the infamous Los Angeles Festival in 1990, which was followed by one in 1993 with Peter Sellars, which wasn't written about too much. Those were huge, and they required so much infrastructure and resources that they just couldn't sustain themselves. When you look at Radar LA, another marker on the map of LA festivals, it was intended to be a biannual festival. But without Olga Garay-English in the city office, it seems the resources totally dried up. I think the difference in what we're doing is that we're working

with the artists to create something from the ground up that is sustainable in the long term, which will grow over time instead of ending abruptly when you run out of money.

I'm also aware of the smaller festivals that are popping up in the art world, like MOCA's [Museum of Contemporary Art] Step and Repeat, though they're working with artists from a very different perspective. I think part of what's energizing Los Angeles right now is Made in LA, an exhibition [during the summer of 2016] at the Hammer Museum, as well as Pacific Standard Time, so art-world-rooted celebrations of local work will hopefully work in our favor.

*That infiltrated the national discourse about the
American art scene in general, and served as a
reminder that there's lineage of West Coast work. It
demonstrated that these artists were here and were
working out of their own line of influence. One*

63

thing that distinguishes curation from producing is that if art curators think about the documentary component, producers are waiting for the newspaper reviewer to show up and give them the quick thumbs-up or thumbs-down, but the art curator produces catalogs and essays to contextualize the work for an audience. Is that piece missing here, in a sense? If we were to take these artists seriously, would either the documentary component or the kind of critical contextualization around their work need to be in place, or would there need to be some kind of mechanism that isn't yet in this nascent scene?

I think so, definitely. We don't have enough writers. We need an army of writers to descend upon Los Angeles to write about the work that's going on. Part of the infrastructure of the LAX Festival is we hire people to document—through writing, video, and photography—every single project that comes through so we are building an archive. And on the front end we hire a photographer to come in and take portraits of every artist that presents, and then we build out mechanisms to tell the audience who these artists are. So we're putting the artist in front of the audience in a public way.

Are you talking about marketing as opposed to arts writing?

Yes, it's marketing, but it also speaks to context. It's important to me that the artists actually have something written about them, as opposed to just a review. So part of building out context for any kind of project is having an understanding of where the artist is coming from and how they came into this project. That's something that I've managed to do with the limited capacity that I have. It's on the web right now, but there's no formal publication. That's just a resource issue for us. But it's my dream to have more of a working loft area that can host residencies, actual time for

experimentation, and a performance library. I look at Artsadmin in London as a great model for how to support more holistically the development of work through access to appropriate research methodologies for artists but also more development support in terms of rehearsal space and commissioning funds. The Live Art Development Agency is another really great institution in the UK that allows artists the space and time to put research into their work. I think that before we even get to the point of having critical response there's a need for artists to have access to performance archives, access to critical response to other pieces, and some incentive to go out and see everything else that's happening. That's going to make the work so much stronger.

It's a crucial element of festivals, and it's often missing because the artists come in for two days and do their show and depart. They can be at a festival with another artist and never manage to see one another, meet, or talk, even if you did catch their show or something like that. Do you make efforts to facilitate conversations among the artists you program? Or to curate a conversation that might take place among artists with similar interests or tendencies?

I do. I think that's a huge flaw in the current festival model. We know it's related to funding and trying to save costs on hotel rooms. After my second-year "sophomore slump," I made a decision to only program local work at least until year five, for the sake of conversation, and to have another marker. After that, we'll probably start to bring in artists from outside of LA again. But with the artists who we present as part of the LAX Festival, it's really clear in even the first meeting that we have an expectation that they see other work that's happening. We give every artist a full festival pass, which I think is common practice, but then we also make sure that they really use that festival pass. My festival is small, and there aren't too many overlapping events, so you can have a full weekend of multiple performance experiences. That's built into the structure, so you don't have to make too many decisions about what to see.

We also hold special events. We do an announcement party late in the summer. I can do this because the artists are local, so everyone can come together, and we announce the full lineup with the artists in the space, and we're able to have conversations with one another at that time. We also do a big public launch party on the first night where all the artists are strongly encouraged to show up. Even the artist portrait situation that I mentioned is a social gathering. We do them all in the same two hours, so everyone shows up, and then they're split up one by one to have their portraits taken, but they meet one another and mingle in between shoots. We try to pull people into the same room as much as possible.

In the future, I hope to create a space for artists to respond to one another's work in a critical and supportive way. We have brought together these weekend conversations as part of the festival, but usually what these conversations turn into is a conversation about what we collectively need to develop in terms of resource in LA. We're not quite past that infrastructure issue to be able to talk about art.

That's the way these conversations naturally want to go.

I think there's a lot of hope here in LA. The artists find ways to support one another out of these conversations. They share studio spaces or storage. There's a lot of sharing that comes out of these conversations; it's still pretty important. I haven't heard artists actually rant about the lack of resources. I probably do that more than they do.

What about the work itself? Do you see any tendencies in the contemporary performance work that you see in Los Angeles? You mentioned that immersive theater is taking hold here, but are there other tendencies that you notice which may be unique to Los Angeles?

Immersive theater is definitely taking hold from the perspective of audience demand. I've read a lot of proposals for new projects, and many of them are dreams of immersive performance. But usually when I curate a festival here in LA, through-lines emerge based on the work itself. Last year a number of conversations around gender identity emerged.

Right now, artists seem to be very concerned with sadness and empathy. Greg Wohead, a Los Angeles artist, is working on a project that was inspired by seeing his Amish grandfather cry once and only once in the time he knew him. These issues around male gender conformity and the ability to show emotion are really resonant with Greg. On the other side, Zoe Aja Moore, who is also developing a project within the CAP UCLA residency platform, is developing a project called *Sad Girl*. It is her way of exploring the cultural

Poor Dog Group's *The Murder Ballad (1938)*, Bootleg Theater, Los Angles, 2013. Photo: Amanda Jane Shank

trends of fangirling and strategic sadness. I think she's trying to tease out why people often use sadness as a cosmetic application within the female identity. Sad girls in popular culture, from Ophelia to Lana Del Rey, are referenced. I'm looking forward to where she goes with it.

That dovetails with a lot of academic work these days in affect theory, that people are exploring these behavioral questions in a cultural application and context.

The other thing I'll say here is the female presence is very dominant in the work that I program and the work that I support. I'm doing my best to promote the work of female artists who are generating work here in LA. The result is a festival that does feel like it's coming out of a more feminine perspective. I think that dealing with issues of the female body and female empowerment is so important now, and has been for some time. I'm still shocked by the misogyny on our stages and at the helm of many of our most critical cultural institutions.

What about politically? In 2013, the city was unveiling big plans for a live/work artist zone here in downtown, and other people were saying, well that sounds great, but this feels like gentrification, and these artists are going to get pushed out, so how are we going to make sure that's not going to happen? How does all this development that you're talking about square with the political desires and expressions of these local artists? Do you notice a political dimension to their thinking? Apart from sheer survival?

Not so much in a way that is directly related to the gentrification of downtown LA, although you now see the outcome of some of that.

I mean, capital has arrived downtown.

It has arrived. And that initiative was called Bringing Back Broadway. I don't know how successful that initiative was in terms of preserving artists' housing. I certainly have not heard of artists relocating to downtown lately, because they're so outpriced.

Artists are actively engaged now in a conversation around gentrification in a neighboring area—Boyle Heights. Because of the skyrocketing prices downtown, artists and galleries have begun to migrate to Boyle Heights, and the long-standing community there is actively fighting the move. The relationship between artists and gentrification is painfully visible in Los Angeles, and current residents of Boyle Heights are demanding that all art galleries in the area leave immediately. The initiative is the Boyle Heights Alliance against Artwashing and Displacement. I don't blame them at all for recognizing the patterns of the city and holding their ground to protect their community. I've seen some work begin to respond to this dynamic, but not too much in performance yet.

More than the political issues of gentrification, artists I'm working with are really engaging with issues around empathy. Having empathy for another's body, caring for bodies in general, especially bodies of color. So you know, the artists seem to be more concerned with political and social issues around race and gender than any other issues. The word *empathy* is coming up again and again.

I think there is a deep concern. The artists that I'm working with also care; they have a deep concern with how they can actually encourage or deepen a capacity for empathy in an audience, and that is in some way related to this hunger that audiences have for immersive theater experiences.

Right. We want an antidote to our empty lives with our little screens and things like that.

Exactly. Which is really contradictory to the virtual reality experience! It's ironic that they are feeding off of immersive theater because virtual reality is not a social form!

All of this seems related to the resurgence of curation, because the root cura originally meant "care." Artists are interested, audiences are interested, and there's supposed to be room for someone to have the role of caring.

I've been working with Kristy Edmunds and Sam Miller recently on a few projects, and both of them have been hugely influential in my work. One project is a research initiative with neuroscientists at UCLA. We're examining the relationship of live performance, memory, creativity, and empathy, specifically, trying to parse how does one, on a college campus, develop a capacity for empathy in a freshman class of students who are not engaging with performance in a way that people have for generations, before we had so much technology interfering.

I consider my job in Los Angeles to be twofold. One is to do everything I can to create conditions for work to reveal itself, and second, I'm invested in work that is shining a light or investigating the most pressing issues of our time. That line is a Kristy Edmunds line, so I'm crediting it to her! This is part of our charge as curators—to create conditions for work to happen but also to ensure that that work is addressing the most pressing issues of our time. We need to be able to engage fully with conversations around empathy, creativity, which are naturally and genetically linked to our memory, our cellular memory, our muscle memory, and our genetic memory. All of these things are tied closely together. That's the work that we have in front of us.

Where do you want to see this in ten years? Still sitting in this loft, working at this scale?

One thing that I have identified through the contrast of working with CAP UCLA is that working at this scale—a scale that I feel to be so important and so satisfying—allows for an intimacy between audience and performance. So I hope, in ten years, to be able to continue working at this scale, but with more infrastructure, support, funding, and audience. And obviously for everything to be wildly successful. The festival will be fifteen years old then, so I hope it isn't too institutionalized at that point. I hope that it's able to sustain itself and still support local artists without growing into a platform that can just present the best of the international work, because plenty of others are already doing that. I hope to retain my commitment to the local.

Boris Charmatz and
Dimitri Chamblas's
À bras-le-corps,
Tate Modern, London,
2015. Photo:
Olivia Hemingway

"Dance Is Dangerous"

Boris Charmatz

Interviewed by Tom Sellar

TOM SELLAR *You started the Musée de la Danse with the celebrated "Manifesto for a Dancing Museum" in 2009. You called for an "infinitely larger diffusion of dance" and a cooperative, permeable "social space for controversy . . . talking and interpretation"[1] and announced that you would temporarily rename the National Choreographic Center of Rennes and Bretagne. But in a way your work as a choreographer has always incorporated curatorial perspectives and practices. Could you talk about that? Was your impulse to bring what you had always done as an artist to an institutional level?*

BORIS CHARMATZ Yes and no. If I look back, I could say that many lines from what we had done before are present, not only from my own work as a choreographer but also what we did at association edna, which was the name of the structure I was working with before Musée de la Danse. Dimitri Chamblas, a dancer, and I founded it. He co-choreographed *À bras-le-corps*, an early duet I did. But then Angèle Le Grand was redirecting association edna with me, and it was really through her input that we developed a lot of early live and visual exhibitions, research projects, books, films, and installations.

Somehow a lot of this could be seen as pre-Musée de la Danse or leading to it, but then Musée de la Danse was really a way to invent an institution. So instead of thinking about projects (and Musée de la Danse is a project) we thought, "What are we going to do for the next two hundred years, let's say? At the same time, what do we do now with this table and two chairs?" It can be poor or very loud, but there was this idea that we would start a museum. The invention of a museum was a good project, because it could really be experimental. Envisioning a museum that collects, we will try to save gestures from the past, recall what should be recalled. We recorded these questions that are important, but nevertheless realized better with other means and other people. We thought, "We're inventing a museum. What would this place be? What would Musée de la Danse (Dancing Museum) be as an institution?"

Also maybe as a new kind of public space where dance could be expanded to a very large scope of perceptions, from reading dance to listening, watching, doing, practicing, learning, and also, you could say, visiting dance, not like a viewer in a theater or an exhibition. You think you're visiting a museum, but dance is visiting you. Maybe you could say the same thing with painting: the paintings are visiting you. You think you're going to see a Richter or Matisse, but maybe the paint-

Theater 47:1 DOI 10.1215/01610775-3710556

ings are looking at you. With dance it's maybe even clearer, because it changes your body, your perception. We wanted a museum where the usual boundaries would be very different: where is the art object, the viewer, the visitors, the curator? There would be a kind of blurriness that was interesting to look for.

In dance we don't have many museums, maybe because the dancer's body is the museum. So what could this be? What kind of project could we do with this idea? Who is the curator? Maybe the dancer is the curator. Who is the guide? Maybe the dancer is the guide. Who or what is the artwork? We're not sure—maybe one dancer is already many artworks. What would a collection in this field be? These questions were not there before Musée de la Danse. To name it was maybe only an inscription on a door. What was behind this door? We didn't know. Somehow I still don't. It was a research project. But to name it like this made everything we had done before different, because now it's about inventing or building an institution.

I had the feeling that my generation, in the 1990s, with Jérôme Bel, Alain Buffard, and Vera Mantero, among others, did a lot of institutional critique in the field of visual art, and maybe also in performance or live art. We had a kind of institutional critique toward what performance and theater are. But somehow to name Musée de la Danse was to shift the institution building or institutional creation, which was very exciting. This was not done at all in other previous projects, even though many things we had done with association edna are part of the Musée de la Danse.

For example, I did an installation called *héâtre-élevision*. It's a strange piece for one viewer at a time with a television. It's a very poor installation, and it was never presented in the US. It's fifty-two minutes long, so every hour you have one viewer. At the end, you have a lineup of viewers, and it's as if you have a full house, but instead of having the full house at eight, you have a full house but each viewer comes later on a fake piano for one hour and it's eight, nine, or ten per day and in one month you have *x* viewers that correspond more or less to one or two theaters. This is really a Musée de la Danse piece, because it can be presented in museums, although you have to take care of it, you can't put it up in a museum where everyone can visit. You have to take an appointment, almost as if you're going to the dentist. It's strange, but I think you could almost say it's a visual arts installation, even if we say it's performance. So this is really a Musée de la Danse project in the sense that it was presented during an exhibition called *Move*, which traveled quite a lot. It's a project that would fit the Musée de la Danse, because it's an installation, but it was done way before.

Then we rewatched what we or other artists had done before with the eyes of Musée de la Danse and made it part of what the institution could be. So there are lots of connections, but also a very clear and specific change that starts with the title and the manifesto.

The name is significant, not just a detail. Putting up a sign announcing this new name in front of the Centre Chorégraphique National caused a lot of confusion.

At the beginning, when we did this, I would talk to people about Musée de la Danse, and a lot of them would say that either it was impossible or a joke, because you don't create a museum for dance. It's OK for one or two months, but then what is your next project? It's a deadly project; it will kill dance. It will become a Madame Tussauds kind of space and fossilize the inventiveness of live dance. Many people had real fears. They weren't just afraid because they didn't like it. They were afraid

Boris Charmatz's
expo zéro, Tate
Modern, London,
2015. Photo:
Olivia Hemingway

because they were in opposition to the idea that we should create a museum for dance. Museum signifies mausoleum, cemetery. Now you can say that it exists. We have done many projects, and we have been invited here or there. The manifesto has been published and republished. But at the beginning, people read the manifesto and said, "Very good project, you will never get the National Choreographic Center, but it's a good project." So this has been a very positive surprise.

And even after you get the center and you persist with this idea, people still thought, "Are you really going to do this?"

I previously did a project called *Bocal*. It was a temporary, one-year-long school, and it was a burning project. We would invent our school, our training, and our exercises. That was the exercise. We didn't invite fantastic teachers from the outside to nourish this school. We were nomadic, and we looked for knowledge. We looked for what pedagogy is, and we invented ourselves as teachers and students. This project really had to do with Musée de

la Danse. It was very different, however, in the sense that we created the school, but it was a burning one. It lasted only one year. Everybody thought, "You want a new school, but we already have schools in France, why would you do a new school?" But it was a burning school, therefore very short. About Musée de la Danse, people said, "It's OK, it will be like *Bocal*, this one-year project for a school. You're naming it 'museum,' but in one year you will do something else." In our head, nevertheless, it was something that is not only a lifelong project but could also go on forever. Even though it might not.

It has a duration, the duration of your contract, right?

Yes. But then, because it's an idea, the Musée de la Danse can move with me somewhere else, or it can be taken over by other people that will disseminate the concept. If you think of the Centre National de la Danse, in Paris, they changed their name last year to say, "We're *centre d'art pour la danse*, we also do exhibitions." Musée de la Danse, as it is now, might end, but its ideas will be disseminated and move elsewhere. I'm not sure we can stop it. It is also related to other projects. We are not alone, although there haven't been many dance museums so far or in the past.

And it has helped to awaken an interest in dance in the art world for many different reasons.

Yes, and I think the context has really changed. When we wrote the manifesto, the first idea for the Musée de la Danse came up maybe eleven years ago, and it was the manager of association edna, Angèle Le Grand, who said, "Why don't we start a Musée de la Danse?" For two years, I thought that was a really stupid idea, it would never happen. A gallery with dance costumes? It didn't make any sense. But then, after two years, I started to understand her idea. It took me some time.

In what I've read from your previous interviews and your own writings, you've talked about museums, museology, expositions, exhibitions, living exhibitions, galleries, display of bodies, but I don't often hear you talk about curation or describe yourself as a curator. You still like the word choreography, *and I've even heard you talk about dramaturgy, a kind of dramaturgy of the body, a living drama.*

I think you're right.

Why?

First, because I always relate myself to being a dancer, which is maybe a fantasy, because I also write, so I could say I'm writer. I make choreographies, so I could say that I'm a choreographer. We programmed exhibitions, so I'm a curator, or a museum director, or a founder. But, since my childhood, dancing is something beyond reason. I said, "My thing is to be a dancer." This didn't only mean spending four hours in the studio. Nobody can

frame being a dancer well. If you enter a taxi, and you say, "I'm a dancer," then the driver is like, "Is it a real job? Are you a faggot?" I don't know how it sounds in English, but you know, ballet dancer, opera? So it's not clear what it is. When you say, "I'm a violinist," maybe people don't know much more about it, but they think it's a real job. To say, "I'm a dancer," somehow it's the way I choose to be a dancer, to be in a social field that is not very recognizable or clear.

And maybe the same happens with the word *curator.* First of all, it sounds really bad in French, *commissaire.* You have the police *commissaire* or the art *commissaire.* It was never the best word. In the Musée de la Danse we do curate, we have exhibitions, but we very often did a lot of collective curatorial practices, or projects. Dance in a museum can bring danger and blurriness. We created *Expo Zéro,* one of the first projects we did with Performa in 2011. We invited ten personalities—architects, philosophers, writers, dancers—and we worked on what the Musée de la Danse could be for each of us. What could the Chamblas Musée de la Danse be? What could your Musée de la Danse be? Jim Fletcher's Musée de la Danse? Or Yvonne Rainer's? What would these be? They reflected the act with their own ideas, in terms of architecture, programming, body work, or what kind of piece they would create.

Then we opened up this discussion, this workshop, to visitors, who visit empty spaces with us—ten guides, but not guides that will necessarily talk and make a visit, but guide toward the vision of what Musée de la Danse could be, and bring the visitors into this idea. It's an empty space where we can do what we want. We can lecture, demonstrate, perform, teach something to the visitors, perform with them, do a live sculpture with the visitor. Everything is open, but we don't use videos, books, computers, music, costumes, props, or theater lights. Nothing.

The idea behind *Expo Zéro* was that the Musée de la Danse, Martina Hochmuth—who works with me—or I select these ten people, sometimes with the help of the institution inviting the project. So there's already three curators, you could say. But actually the main idea of *Expo Zéro* is for these ten people to be the curators of an exhibition, and they are their own curators. So, instead of having one curator for many artworks, you have ten curators for no artworks. You have to invent the artworks, and if you stop, there's no artwork.

I like the idea that I'm not the curator of these exhibitions, even though I'm a kind of curator of *Expo Zéro*. My original idea was that we would have ten curators, therefore ten displays. If you follow me, you have an idea of Musée de la Danse that is very different than if you follow Faustin Linyekula, a Congolese choreographer. You follow him you will see how he would like to put Warhol objects/artworks in the museum. So, if you follow him, you have a completely different idea of what the Musée de la Danse is or could be than if you follow Tim Etchells, me, or someone else. This is why I didn't name myself a curator, because this position was supposed to be split, disseminated, and reworked. But yes, I'm a curator, even though I don't use the term that much. Maybe because I work with real curators sometimes.

You have worked with Catherine Wood, at Tate Modern in London.

Yes, Catherine Wood. I don't have a doubt about her being a curator. My doubt is really about myself being a curator, in the sense of how to relate to the history of curatorial approaches. I'm an artist and perhaps have some diagonal ideas about curation, but I don't know very important exhibitions, for example, from the history of art in the twentieth century.

In the classical sense.

Yes, and I respect that. I'm not saying that we don't need curators.

When I talk to the visual arts curators, they are sometimes skeptical of people in performing arts who call their work curation. Where's the catalog essay? Or where is the research process? Where is the documentation?

I must say that when we started the Musée de la Danse the first thing we thought of was the space of a museum, a new kind of space for dance, adapted to it. It is a museum, but there's a theater and a school inside. We can use the spaces for exhibiting not only things but also bodies. The more we worked, the clearer it was that a museum is more than the white cube, the Frank Gehry, the scopic display. Museums actually produce a lot of catalogs, research, and pedagogy. And this could be even more important in the end, because almost no theater publishes anything. When they do, it's only on the occasion of an anniversary, because it's not really part of what a theater does. There's one exception among twenty, and usually you don't read it—you put it on the shelf. We also make the programs, but they mainly serve to bring people in. So it's more about communication, and, of course, museums are also concerned about bringing in as many visitors as they can.

But going back to Catherine Wood, she wrote a book about Yvonne Rainer, *The Mind Is a Muscle* [2007]. That's an example of a text that I want to keep and to read. It's challenging and, although I'm not saying it is more interesting than seeing Yvonne Rainer's work, it could be of equal importance in a sense. In the field of dance, and maybe live art in general, not many theater directors have the capacity to be writers, researchers, and programmers. You are a programmer, period. So, basically, you have to select the best shows of

Boris Charmatz's
*20 Dancers for the
XX Century*, Tate
Modern, London,
2015. Photo:
Joe Humphrys

the best artists for your program, but the deep questions of the display, the collection, and the history remain unanswered. Maybe some programmers have these concerns, of course, but it's not the tradition. In any museum you do symposiums, lecture series, and it's normal that a curator is organizing a symposium or picture series and she herself speaks during it. It would be abnormal if she didn't have her own intervention. In a theater, it would be very strange, even if there were a lecture series or talk, for the theater director to speak, because traditionally we are not researchers, scholars, curators, or programmers. And this is something that I admire. You can also criticize it, but it's something we need to be inspired by.

This leads to my next question: to what extent was your inspiration drawn from a discourse on contemporary dance, and to what extent did you intervene in the discourse, make a change in it through this institution?

I would like to have an answer that is not too complex or twisted. We have presented at MOMA or Tate, but, in fact, we founded the Musée de la Danse almost in opposition to the art museums. Some choreographers, especially the dry, conceptual ones, were interested in working in museums, because the discourse level would be higher, the context more interesting, and the lenses through which to see the work would be more appealing than the dance festival lenses or the dance annual season. But we started Musée de la Danse in opposition to that way of thinking. We would create a museum for ourselves and be our own masters. I am not saying that we are not interested in the history of visual art. But we are definitely interested in the history of dance, and we want to bring Mike Kelley and Viennese Actionism into it, or see films as choreography. That would really help enlarge the perception of what the dance field can be.

There was a moment for Tino Sehgal, for example, where he had to put on the disguise of the visual artist. Even though he is a dancer, doing performative situations, he has to adopt the persona of the visual artist who can sell his products, because you can reproduce a sculpture or a film. In our case, creating the Musée de la Danse was a way to say that we don't need to pretend we are not dancers in order to be taken seriously as artists. We are dancers, but dancers have a lot to teach, to say about what a collection can be or how memory functions. Dance also has another history of how to redo things. It is not necessarily a better history or a better way to deal with the past, but it is another kind of tradition, another array of tools. Again, where is the artwork located? It is very different from where painting is located, so I never felt that I have a debt toward the work of art, and I still don't. Often it comes from economy, very different economies, so sometimes one becomes the slave of the other one. There's a power relation, but if you push the economic frames that make visual art or dance, they have a lot in common and are nourishing each other. The only problem is that, after fifty years of work, Bruce Nauman has fifty books that you can still find, whereas Simone Forti after fifty years (and she actually did publish) has four books, and you can't even find them anymore. That is the main difference.

Sometimes Musée de la Danse has made these lineages you describe essential components of a work. For example, in the project called Flip Book, *you ask professional dancers to repeat choreography from [Merce] Cunningham, in relation to photographic collections, and then reinterpret it. In a way these projects make explicit, or central, what has always been important in dance, which is these lineages, mentorships, relationships between two bodies that are sharing time in a studio, transmitting to one another.*

I must say that with this Cunningham project there is a lineage between Cunningham the performer that is framed as a short circuit, because I didn't dance with him, even if I would have liked to. I'm not a follower, and he wouldn't at all recognize us. Somehow, with Musée de la Danse—and even before—we did a lot of things, for example, with butoh. I don't know much about Cunningham, so we picked up a book. He's absent, working in his studio, because when we started this project he was still alive, doing his next project. We are in Berlin, I'm with students, they are bored, and they know nothing about Merce Cunningham, Andy Warhol, Robert Rauschenberg, or John Cage. What can we do? He's not there. He's ninety or eighty-nine, and he's not going to come and teach us.

Within the dance tradition, we would invite Cunningham, and he would come and teach us his technique. But I thought, "No, we have this very strange book from the archivist, David Vaughan, and we have these pictures." In the dance field, pictures are not dance, because they are fixed and we are in movement; they are flat and we are 3D. But I was saying "It's already dance, because you connect two pictures, and they are already a Cunningham dance." It's not the one he invented; he invented what is inside the pictures. But it's our turn now to recreate what exists between these two pictures. So somehow there is a lineage, in the sense that we connect to Cunningham. At the same time, there's also a total break, rupture, or invention of a lineage that doesn't exist. And then, when you see people performing the Cunningham project, you think you will see fifty years of dance, because that's what we do—it's a book with five decades of dance from beginning to end. You end up seeing the history of the body doing it. So you think you will see some modern American dance—and you partly do, because there is something purely connected to that, to Cunningham's heritage—but you witness something that has to do with your history, even with a larger scale than Cunningham's history, because the viewers see that you did some years in some ballet, long ago, or you never danced but you always wanted to jump and you're amazing at it.

So we use the history of dance to show another people's own history. And, usually, when you work with nondancers, you work with them based on their own skills. You can walk or sit down, but you like to move on the dance floor, so we start from what you can do. With this project, however, we start from what we can't do, since trying something foreign that comes from the past reveals more of who you are than doing something you already know. In that sense, you get to know more about the history of the dancers in *Flip Book*, a project that is done with amateurs, than with the real Cunningham dancers, who are trained to execute his work and to be a part of the company, which means you don't see them anymore as individuals who, for example, danced hip-hop for ten years. Even if they did, you see Cunningham dancers. In our project, nevertheless, we work with as many people as possible, so then you see a person who was educated in Cape Verde, and you still detect the Cape Verdean kind of elements in Cunningham's choreographies.

At the same time, you could say it's curation, because it's the rearrangement of a series of existing artworks in a new creation, a new exposition.

Yes, I think it is. We did some projects where we would relate to this lineage you were mentioning in the Cunningham project, *Flip Book*. We also we did a project that I really loved called *Rebutô*—re-butô—which we invited many artists to. The name of the project is a game in French: *rebutant*, which means dis-gusting. *Rebutô* is a game. It means "never again" or "disgusting butô," because *rebutant* describes something you don't want to touch. We invited Xavier Le Roy for the project, because he had once told me that to become a butoh dancer you don't need five years in Japan practicing with a master. You just need two hours. I wrote him a letter, and he accepted. He worked much more than two hours, but then, during the performance, which lasted two hours, he became a butoh dancer. But it's Xavier Le Roy! I really liked this project with the Musée de la Danse, because it proposed a clear short-circuit connection with history, or past references. When we started the Musée de la Danse, our intention was not to look back at the 1960s, Isadora Duncan, or even at Charlie Chaplin. We created a museum, but we wanted to invent. What would this invention be? If it had to do with Cunningham, great, but if it didn't, it would be great as well or even better. The fact is we started a museum for now, for what is urgent now. And maybe in the future we'll look at it as history. But we didn't want the Musée de la Danse to be connected only to rethinking archive and history or reinventing memory.

Do you want to give an example of a project that is a performance of contemporaneity?

Sure. My piece *Levée des conflits* (*Suspension of Conflicts*) was very connected to the Musée de la Danse and not at all connected to the past or classical references. I had this desire for a piece in which dancers would move a lot, but the main perception of the piece would be that it would stay completely immobile, stabile. So we would do a sculpture where, in three seconds, you would see all the movements of a given dance piece. You basically saw everything that is usually given little by little in a dance piece, because you have the beginning, the middle moment (where they start jumping), and the end (where they hug). The idea was that, in three seconds, you can see it all, like a sculpture or an installation in an exhibition.

There is in the piece a strange canon system. The dancers are not just repeating the same movement for two hours—so that each viewer sees the same movements at the same time—but are also changing movements. So I have one movement, and I pass it on to you. Then I take over the movement of the dancer in front of me, and so on. For the viewer, the piece doesn't move—it looks like stone—but the dancers are dancing in canon, like in "Frère Jacques." In "Frère Jacques" you sing "dormez-vous," but as a listener you always hear "Frère Jacques," because it's being sung by different voices. Our piece was a complex take on that.

This was really a Musée de la Danse idea, because it was about recreating a sculpture, a picture, or a fixed object that is completely defined, immobile even, but it worked through a process of performativity that is our dramaturgy. You could still draw a line between this work and some gestures from the past, but the idea was not to rethink butoh, or work from Yvonne Rainer's similar concepts. I mentioned my own work, but we have collaborated with many artists at the Musée de la Danse. For instance, a lot of the participants experimented and developed ideas for *Expo Zéro*. Afterward, it became their own work, which could be the start of some project that was not looking back at something that already existed.

You said once that the potentiality of a Musée de la Danse is the kind of animating force that always informs each project. What could happen in a Musée de la Danse if we had one? But now you've been doing this for a while. It's been how many years?

Seven.

That continues to drive projects. Can you talk about that, the kind of inspiration to a potential, versus what is happening in actuality?

The truth is that, in a way, we accumulate. A lot of our exhibitions or projects are more like a protocol of work. So they are not like a Matisse exhibition that travels. Even in a Matisse exhibition, the display would be different in the Centre Pompidou in Beaubourg than somewhere else. An exhibition is always changing, although you can take it and remount it. On the contrary, our exhibitions and projects are closely linked to their context. So, even if we redo *Expo Zéro* next year in Poland, it will not be at all the same *Expo Zéro* that we did in New York.

To me, the Musée de la Danse is an interesting project as long as it's experimental and leads us somewhere. The moment it becomes a habit, I'll stop, probably because I'm an artist and my main quality isn't to theorize or accumulate treasures. I love the idea that we do have a collection, but without an acquisition budget. We have it, but it's random, and some pieces are real, in the sense that you open the books in our storage room and you have an artwork. It could be a score, an idea, or a film. Some things have been deposited, but we don't own them. I like that we have a collection but it's not a treasure that we can just sell.

I have the feeling that we have to go on, and, if the question of the collection is not important anymore, either Musée de la Danse has to shift, or we have to end it. One of the very recent developments, which I would never have imagined seven years ago, is rethinking public spaces, and art for public spaces. Since the beginning we've been looking for the ideal architecture for Musée de la Danse, because we don't have it in Rennes.

Fabrice Mazliah's
Six potentialités,
Fous de danse,
Esplanade
Charles-de-Gaulle,
Rennes, 2016. Photo:
Richard Louvet

We are in a theater, and we have to beg to perform here. We have studio spaces, which we transform into exhibition spaces, but we feel constrained by the actual spaces. We have also taken over other kinds of spaces like Tate Modern, for one weekend. It has the best architecture you could think of. But what became clearer to us is that we were interested in Tate Modern as a museum. If you think about Tate Modern, everyone can enter. There's the Turbine Hall at the center, Tate's most symbolic space. When they started Tate Modern, they created another kind of Gehry white cube but with a collection. And the big change that Tate Modern brought on was this Turbine Hall where you don't know what will happen, or how to exhibit there. In that sense, the museum shifted significantly the notion of public space, because it's free, and you can enter and have a picnic in the Turbine Hall. Working with museums through the project of the Musée de la Danse has made me think

more and more about public spaces, not only in the sense of inventing our architecture for a public space but also going to an empty public square, with no walls, and realizing that maybe this is the best architecture for the Musée de la Danse. Seven years ago, I would never have said this. We've done things in a huge public square, here in Rennes . . .

Place Charles de Gaulle?

Yes, which is one hundred by one hundred and twenty meters. It's very big and completely empty. Working there with the Musée de la Danse, we thought, "This is where we have to work. This is a new kind of project we have to do." If we want to exhibit anything, we do it here. The exhibition happens here. Three weeks, one hour, ten minutes. However, in this empty space, people are passing by anyway, so the movement is already there. It might be raining, but someone is crossing for sure, so you already have movement, and, because it's embedded in the city, there are people that, with or without reason, are there. If it becomes an art space, for one day, three months, or one year, the kind of art we can do is very different from the art we would create here [inside]. This really became for us the guiding line for what we can do in public spaces. Moreover, in the public spaces there are—especially today—many more soldiers than dancers. Of course, with the recent events [the Bataclan terrorist attack] in Paris, this imbalance between armed soldiers or policemen and unarmed dancers increased. I'm not saying we should turn policemen into dancers, but I still think the public space is one of the major problems of contemporary life. It used to be free, but it became a space for advertisement that gets privatized for corporate events, instead of remaining a place where we can live together. It is also regulated by socioeconomic codes: you don't cross because you're from that suburb, you are dressed like this, you wear a veil. It's not a place for people to meet, but actually a place for people not to meet. Therefore, I think we have to rethink the ways in which we move together and use dance as a medium to transform. It's urgent.

It's a problem for the culture section in general also, because there's an exclusivity. It's always in the city center. How to connect this form of culture with people who are living in outer suburbs?

Yes, and I think that, more than creating a superficial idea of collectivity, we have to foster dissent or, in other words, a consensus around the notion that we also need dissent. The public space is a place for gathering, but it's also a place where you can do hardcore art that maybe some people won't like. We can have crazy artists. It's OK. Dissent is also part of our identity, our cultural understanding, and I think—again as a dancer—that dance is the right medium to bring it up, because

it's intuitive. You're in front of a child, and he or she starts dancing. You can go very quickly from participatory projects to looking at pieces or exhibiting them. Because you change your posture, you can quickly go from being the performer to being the guide or the viewer. In dance, I have sneakers, but you also have sneakers, so who says you're not the choreographer? Honestly, nobody. I like that idea that dance is the right medium to modify our experience of the public space, which is our focus for the next three years. This is something I could never have thought of seven years ago. The Musée de la Danse has transformed my perspective, because now I think the best architecture is to have none. And I'm really excited to play with *météo* [weather] conditions. In one year we'll be tired maybe, but so far so good.

Another thing that is extremely interesting about the Musée de la Danse is the holistic integration of pedagogy into the project. In a lot of institutions, even very contemporary ones, this needs to be done in order to get public money or funds and it's an afterthought. They designate somebody to do it, who's not really central to the organization. But here, it's very much the center of what you do. The artists and yourself are students in some sense. Can you talk about that?

It's a demand more in dance than in visual art institutions. Any choreographer or dancer has to do pedagogy and activities for amateurs nowadays. If you are the director of a choreographic center, you have to do activities in schools, prisons, and so on, which is problematic, because you don't create good art if you are obliged to do it. It would be great if artists and curators didn't have to do it, if they don't feel like it, because it's also great to have museums where there's not talking visits. Empty museums are great. Now we are so happy to have museums full with people. I want the empty museum that Thomas Bernhard described, where you go alone every Sunday, nobody is there, and you are alone in front of a painting, to be possible. Although pedagogy is central to the Musée de la Danse, I don't think that all dance institutions should have a focus on pedagogy. There were a lot of exhibitions where dancers were used to perform Marina Abramović's pieces, but I don't know what the gesture means. You're in front of an Abramović artwork, and the dancer is repeating the same thing. He's not a dancer anymore. He's embodying this artwork, which is OK. But if you think, "What can a dancer bring to an exhibition?," this isn't it. Because he can bring the fact that he is many artworks and he's there, but he could be somewhere else. A sculpture, an installation, a film, or a web project doesn't move by itself. Dance is dangerous. You think you're in front of an artwork, but it's actually moving elsewhere. You think it's a Tino Sehgal, but it's not. Dancers can be identified with art, one specific artwork or author, but they become something else. This is where pedagogy is important for us, in this shift of positions. It's not that I dislike the fact that museums have a guard, security people, pedagogy people . . .

Of course, in twenty years we will have an archivist and a guide. Right now, we are a baby museum. We don't have the means to have a security guy, so this means the dancer is able to move too. It's really challenging to go from pedagogy to hardcore performance. To move from guiding, talking, and lecturing to doing. A visitor can think he or she is visiting Musée de la Danse, but it's like a trap, and you end up doing a dance class. There's also something about where the artwork is that's the crucial point for me. You come into Musée de la Danse, you learn this *Flip Book*, you learn a project, and after ten days or two hours you leave, and where's the artwork? It's basically inside. I really like this idea that Musée de la Danse doesn't own anything. In the

end you still have the book that is older and older, or more fragile and more fragile, but art being created is then going back home with the visitors. I think it's a relevant idea for art through dance. This is why we do it. I think pedagogy in a large sense, not in terms of masters and disciples or schools, is something we need—thinking through dance, thinking through our own practice. And then visitors thinking through their own visit. And, how to relate the art space and the social space? I think that Musée de la Danse could do this more easily than any other museum.

Ironically, it's one of the classical functions of curation, to disseminate to the public the theory or context.

Sure. But I love the lecture series with the exhibitions at MOMA. Somehow at Musée de la Danse that doesn't even feel like a big decision. We do the lecture series, and the performance and the exhibition are one. Maybe the symposium is the core. I'm thinking MOMA, but it's not for the visitors. They would be bored. It's better to have a clean white cube with the very well-lit artwork, a masterpiece. But at Musée de la Danse we don't have the masterwork or the Trisha Brown groupies. We don't own the artwork. We don't have the money to present it, and we don't have the space. We have the idea of what it was or how you could do it. This puts the pedagogy inside the art as art, and not just pedagogy to support the art. It has been creative so far, but I'm not sure about the future. I'm not sure about what we've done. I'm not sure about what we'll do. We don't have all the keys that could help a museum, because basically our keys are specific to our project. If you think about the big collections of the art institutions, I'm not sure. What we could do with Musée de la Danse with the help of visual artists who were accepting is that dancers could move the

Boris Charmatz and
Dimitri Chamblas's
À bras-le-corps, 2015.
Photo:
Olivia Hemingway

artwork without having white gloves or with the risk of destroying one, and this is exactly what you can't do, should never do within a traditional institution. We are not a model to be followed. Our school, *Bocal*, was a burning school. Of course, you can be inspired by it, great, but I would never recommend reproducing it, because it was hell. And if you want to be sustainable, you don't do a burning school. You have to be sure that the next day the students are coming back healthy and well taken care of. So you don't do a crazy project, or as crazy as what we are able to do.

I would like to ask you about this archive. You said you don't want a collection in any conventional sense. It's a living archive in the body. At the same time, there's great value, as we see from this representation, in repertoire, in coming back, returning to pieces, seeing them again, twenty years later, measuring the distance from before. How do we reconcile these things? It's a problem in dance, which is an ephemeral form where everything disappears. Is there a responsibility of the museum to counter this ephemerality?

Sure. Somehow this is where I'm not a spectacle fan. Of course I like new artworks. I like premieres, but I don't revere the premiere. I love it one hundred times later—the getting old into it. For Musée de la Danse it is easier to say, "We do this piece, and, of course, it's twenty years old." Nobody would say, "Why would you do an old piece?" because it's Musée de la Danse. But I would do it even without Musée de la Danse. In the field of classical music, you always reperform Beethoven, Bach, and Tchaikovsky. But then where is the new work? It's 5 percent of what musicians are doing. Then you have a big problem. But I would say that in the dance field, so far, the rethinking Nijinsky, the redoing old pieces, the playing repertoire is really limited compared to doing a new work every year. If a dance is too old, put in a new, younger dancer. This is still dominant.

If everybody was doing repertoire all the time and no more new creations, I would say, "Forget this." But, so far, in this fight between, let's say, looking again at that old stuff or doing new stuff, in contemporary dance, as the name says, every year we do a new piece. If you do a new piece, we are still interested. If it's an old piece we, we don't present it. Whereas I think we have a heritage that is great to see again and again. Because some pieces, they were unnoticed twenty years ago, but they should be noticed. Perhaps if you saw a piece in its original time you would have seen many articles talking about nudity. Of course, now some people would still talk about nudity, but the impact is not on nudity at all. It could even be a counterreaction, like, "Ah, again!" But there was maybe a gap between the 1970s and 1990s. There was Jérôme. Not only nudity, but super interesting projects using nudity as a cultural tool, not nudity as an expressive act, but nudity as a way to enter the cultural field, the history of culture. So not a naive, let's say, nakedness, but a very precise cultural choice. Now, twenty years later, nudity is not the point anymore. This means that you can focus on other things, and I really like that. For the artists themselves, some movements you do years ago and you think, "It's such good movement and I created for this reason," and then twenty years later you're like, "Why did I do this?" But maybe the "How to do this?" becomes more important than the thing, the movement itself. I really like how we relate to old movement.

What about at the institutional level? Musée de la Danse is an institution of experimentation, and experimentation means failure a lot of the time. How do you process failure? Is there a documentation where you can evaluate and say, "OK, this was wrong for this reason"?

Yes. By dance world standards, we are really rich. We have a choreographic center, you know? But if you compare our museum to others, we are one of the poorest. We can't hire an archivist. We have to do things ourselves. We try to archive as much as we can,

but I must admit that it's not easy. There are some projects, like *Flip Book*, that you can film and they look great. But *Expo Zéro* and some of the most important projects are not easily archived, because a lot happens between the speech and the act. You can select some texts, publish something, or take pictures, but it doesn't turn out so great. A lot of what we do happens within the mental space, in the head of the viewer and the artist. It makes the art happen, but it's not easily archived.

We have Gilles Amalvi, a writer, who writes about almost every project we do, and we try to document on film and archive it. But with association edna, we were able to do little films that are maybe more impressive, because that was the only thing we would do. With the Musée de la Danse, we do many things, but then it's harder to follow up and document all the projects. We have also chosen to be more on the side of creating than stabilizing our own activity. It was a choice, because we are not big enough to do everything with the same standards of quality. So we hope that people like Catherine Wood and many others, or the people who have the eyes and the brain to rethink what we are doing, can extract from that what the essence of our projects is. We are very active and we try as much as we can, but I know we are not as good as we could be. We hope that people who are interested and researchers come. We have an archive that they can dig into and make something of. After all, we have done some projects that still exist: we did film, web installations, and interactive video from the first two editions of *Expo Zéro*. It's all right, for now. *C'est pas mal.*

Are you going to do Fous de Danse *again?*

Yes, I would like to do it. I really like the last projects we've done, the transformative formats. In *Fous de Danse*, which has a very specific format, the idea is that you go from

warm-up to transmission, to instant choreography, to real professional choreography,
and then to social dancing. It's about having
a dance experience that is always falling into
another format. It's collective, but it shifts
from the exhibition to the performance, from
performance to transmission, from transmission to social dancing, to theory, to lectures,
and so on. But this doesn't take place as one
project. Usually you do the dance class here,
the performance there, the lecture over there,
and the groups that are seeing, looking, doing
are different from one another. There's the
dancer, the students, the viewers, and some
of them mingle, but it's still very divided. It's
a completely transformative experience, it's
burning and I want to do more of that. We
then have a project in Berlin, because we'll
be associate artists of the Volksbühne for five
years. We are really busy thinking about what
this project will be, how much the Musée de
la Danse can or cannot be within the Volksbühne, because that theater is another frame.
If you think about the name—Volksbühne,
"the stage of the people"—you don't need to
add the Musée de la Danse to it. It's enough.
So, how do we work? How can we do a
jumelage? In Europe you have this tradition
of connecting one city to another and then
you do exchanges. It's a postwar initiative.
It's usually a very poor program, for political purposes only, but could we do an artistic
jumelage Rennes–Berlin? Or what is needed
in Berlin? I'm busy with that, for sure. I don't
know yet what we'll do, but I'm very excited
by these possibilities.

NOTE

1. Boris Charmatz, "Manifesto for a Dancing Museum," in *Danse: An Anthology*, ed.
Noémie Solomon (Dijon, France: Les presses du réel, 2014), 233–34.

Day 47.
Image by the artist

Portfolio

Worth the Review

Kenneth Collins

The *New York Times* has a slogan: "All the news that's fit to print." But as a theater maker in New York City, the inclusivity, in terms of discourse on contemporary performance, has perpetually eluded me. I have consequently always felt somewhat divorced from the world of theater painted in the pages of the *New York Times*, even though the paper has regularly written favorably about my work over the years.

In *The Autobiography of Alice B. Toklas*, Gertrude Stein wrote, "I always say that you cannot . . . tell what an object really is until you dust it every day."[1] So you could say that I became absorbed by the idea of dusting off the theater section of the *New York Times* each day in an attempt to understand a thing that I thought should be clear to me but wasn't. If the *New York Times* is the lens through which the general public views, understands, and evaluates theater, I started to wonder, is it a clean lens or a funhouse mirror?

The *New York Times* is often referred to as our "paper of record," and there is no question that it defines the field of theater for many of its readers. Few if any sources for theater reviews in this country carry the same voice of authority. So it should come as no surprise that all of the artists and producers that I know hope to receive a great review from the *New York Times*. Yet, to be honest, I don't know many in my community who actually seem to respect the quality of discourse taking place in the paper when it comes to contemporary performance. In fact, I often hear big complaints about it. The *New York Times* reviews are repeatedly criticized for being condescending, harsh, unproductive, or, at times, even basking in their own cleverness. Some of the worst of this gets thrown at young artists who are just getting their start. But equally troubling is that there seems to be an overall conventional bias in the paper when it comes to deciding what makes good "theater." There are exceptions, but they tend to prove the rule.

Many artists and organizations I know seem to care only so much about the reviews, because they look at them as a form of free advertising. A good review means

Theater 47:1   DOI 10.1215/01610775-3710568

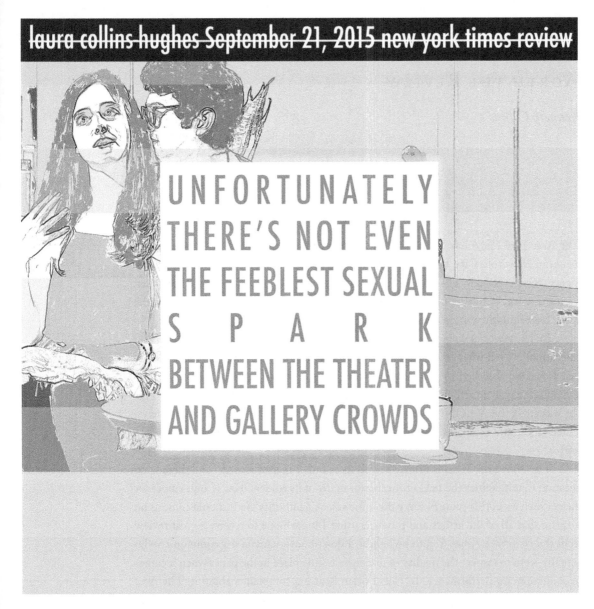

laura collins hughes September 21, 2015 new york times review

UNFORTUNATELY THERE'S NOT EVEN THE FEEBLEST SEXUAL S P A R K BETWEEN THE THEATER AND GALLERY CROWDS

Day 100.
Image by the artist

(perhaps) greater ticket sales. Unfortunately, with this perspective, the discourse and commentary in the review itself can begin to feel almost beside the point when speaking to producers, press representatives, or marketing staff. Instead, the review is treated simply as a source text to be bent and distorted every which way possible in order to find a great pull quote that can help market the production.

If you look closely at some of the pull quotes, it's actually funny the way that things get yanked out and decontextualized to market the work. Sometimes it is

Day 113.
Image by the artist

really forced, just because there is a wonderful seal of approval to be had if you can put "—*New York Times*" after a quote. So I thought, what if I were to pull quotes from the paper instead to say all these absurd, outrageous things about theater, "—*New York Times*"?

    In the summer of 2015, I began posting these quotes from the theater reviews on Instagram and Facebook. For an entire year, I created one erasure-based text each day from a single *New York Times* review, using only words that appeared in the review

ben brantley October 18, 2015 new york times review

CORPSES FRESHLY RISEN FROM THEIR GRAVES AREN'T USUALLY AS D E A D AS SHAKESPEARE IN THE THEATER

Day 145.
Image by the artist

and only in the strict chronological order in which they appeared but omitting as many words as necessary to bend the language of the paper to my liking. Once I started the project, I never skipped a single review.

I quickly realized just how many reviews were being published each day in the *New York Times*—arguably more than are "fit to print." And to see how often some critics are publishing—it's relentless! I have to admit, I can't imagine being in that job and having to write that many reviews on that sort of a regular schedule. What toll does that have on you as a spectator and critic? I could barely keep up with my job of cutting the reviews into these dinky blurbs.

ken jaworowski October 23, 2015 new york times review

I CAN'T SAY I RECOMMEND STORYTELLING IN THE THEATER

After some time working on the quotes, I became genuinely fascinated by the press photos that are published with each review and began reworking these images, too, in a very rough way. The images felt somewhat like paintings, and I used them to surround my quotes. I think the photos are engaging because they carry a bias all their own. On the whole, they focus on characters who are relating to one another in a way that privileges the view of theater as a form of storytelling. Even in images of postdramatic theater, the photos published in the *New York Times* often signal a more conventional dramaturgy than what is actually present in the work onstage.

Day 159.
Image by the artist

THEATER IS A ROOM DARKENED FOR LOVERS OF CLASS-BASED CONDESCENSION AND CONTEMPORARY REALISM

Day 215.
Image by the artist

I began this project without any preconceived notions about what it was going to be. The first couple of posts were far more abstract—almost stream-of-consciousness—compared with the style that I eventually settled on. But pretty early on, the project became more of an institutional critique, which is a form of art that doesn't really have much of a presence in the theater.

As someone who is used to a collaborative process, it was strange to work in a vacuum, posting on Instagram each day. But I received some great responses in the form of e-mails, text messages, and social media comments along the way. In one instance,

neil genzlinger February 01, 2016 new york times review

GOOD THEATER IS NOT LIVE TV

Day 310.
Image by the artist

after I posted my version of a review of his show on Instagram, Jeremy Barker reposted the image on Facebook and wrote, "If you haven't seen this, we're all at Sister Sylvester quite proud to be part of Kenneth Collins's conceptual pop art poetry project of *NY Times* theater reviews. It's frankly the thing that makes the review worth it." Echoing a sentiment similar to what started me on this project, Shoshona Currier, director of performing arts for the Chicago Department of Cultural Affairs and Special Events, commented on Facebook on day 364 of this project, "I feel like the truly rigorous part of this project was actually reading this many *New York Times* theater reviews. Blurgh."

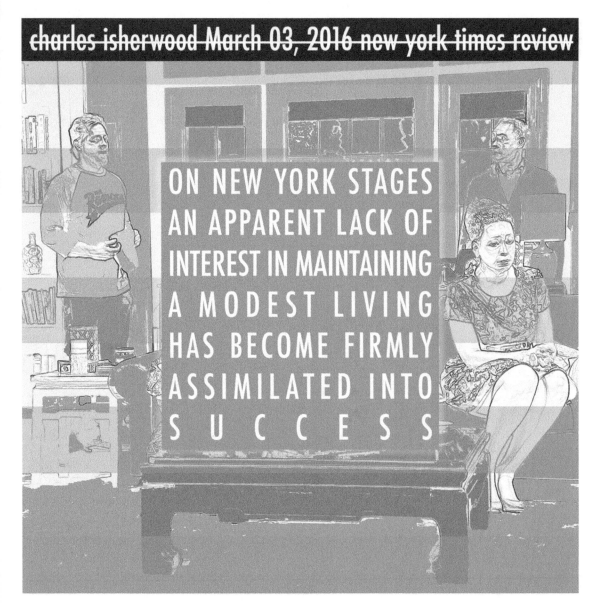

charles isherwood March 03, 2016 new york times review

ON NEW YORK STAGES
AN APPARENT LACK OF
INTEREST IN MAINTAINING
A MODEST LIVING
HAS BECOME FIRMLY
ASSIMILATED INTO
S U C C E S S

Day 362.
Image by the artist

I think of the 365 Instagram quotes as playful appropriations that raise questions (if only for myself) about how the *New York Times* is framing success and failure in the world of theater. The posts ask the questions: Who are these reviews written for? What is the mandate? I tried to channel the hostility and silliness found in some of the reviews into a different form in order to bring their tone into relief, to look at the trends in the language and logic, to put it on its head. How are we thinking about what makes good theater? And who gets to decide?

All 365 reviews can be found on Instagram @temporarydistortion.

NOTE

1. Gertrude Stein, F. W. Dupee, and Carl Van Vechten, *Selected Writings of Gertrude Stein* (New York: Modern Library, 1962), 106.

"Show Me The
World," Haus der
Kunst, Munich, 2015.
Photo: Stefan Loeber

Sigrid Gareis and Tilmann Broszat

Translated by Lisa Jeschke

How to Show Worlds?

Since the end of the 1980s, there have been extensive discussions in the visual arts of how and in what form international art and artists can be presented in a timely way. In 1989, the exhibition Magiciens de la Terre, held at the Centre Georges Pompidou and the Grande Halle de la Villette in Paris, was the first to represent in equal numbers and in the framework of a unified presentation Western and non-Western artists, and in 2001–2 *documentaii* as curated by Okwui Enwezor sustainably introduced postcolonial debates into the art world. In the visual arts, rising numbers of *biennales* and art fairs around the globe continue to intensify complex discussions concerning a "global contemporary" and curatorial responses.

In the performing arts, too, we can observe from the 1990s onward an increase in invitations to productions from non-Western countries and in programs centered on specific countries and regions on the part of the big international festivals of the Western hemisphere (from the mid-1990s onward China is often a focal point; from 2010 onward the Arab Spring). Nevertheless, there has been little discussion as yet concerning the theory, methodology, practice, and, in particular, ethical framework of curating and organizing in a globally linked world.

In 2015, the multipart project "Show Me the World," taking place in a number of cities, was the first to focus on questions related to curation in an international context—not least concerning exoticization in curatorial practices, transcultural curatorial methods, a global ethics of event organization, hegemonic or horizontal relations in the presentation of art, and ethno- or Eurocentrism in contemporary festival and theater circuits.

Six invited curators from four different continents—Rolf Abderhalden (Bogotá), Jelili Atiku (Lagos), Anja Dirks (Fribourg), Ahmed El Attar (Cairo), Judy Hussie-Taylor (New York), and Ong Keng Sen (Singapore)—encountered one another initially

Theater 47:1   DOI 10.1215/01610775-3710453

"Show Me The World," Munich, 2015. Photo: Stefan Loeber

in pairs to exchange methodologies concerning their regionally specific curatorial practices; this was facilitated by a number of local Goethe Institutes. In the spring of 2015, they were then invited to Mülheim for a first public exchange, at this point in collaboration with the Impulse Theater Festival and the KULTURsekretariat North Rhine-Westfalia.

On October 24–26, a concluding project symposium took place at the SPIELART Festival in Munich. Prestigious international academics and curators provided an intensive program of presentations, discussions, and workshops: the six curators co-organizing the symposium introduced curating and event-organizing practices in so-called area studies, leading into discussions with renowned colleagues, among them Adrian Heathfield (London), André Lepecki (New York/Rio de Janeiro), Jay Pather (Cape Town), and Suely Rolnik (São Paulo), most of whom contribute an article to this issue of *Theater*.

A university seminar at Ludwig Maximilians University of Munich complemented the program.

The project is extensively documented on the SPIELART homepage (spielart.org /showmetheworld); important theoretical contributions to the symposium have been expanded for this issue. Here we address in cursory form some practice-orientated results emerging from the symposium and seminar, in particular, methodological questions concerning continued "othering" and Eurocentrism in the program design of festivals and institutions.

To do justice to the demands of transculturalism, we can learn from the visual arts in multiple ways. Many exhibitions and *biennales* are consciously conceptualized collectively by persons from a variety of cultural backgrounds. In curatorial decision making, this not only generally establishes a dialogical principle of culture but also balances the usually authoritative position of programming as conducted by a single person.

As a consequence, a first contact zone is established, proposed by ethnologist James Clifford as a mediation model for museums in reference to the terminology of literary scholar Mary Louise Pratt.[2] Museums are to be constructed as negotiating spaces in which different cultural and social positions collide and find discussion and controversy, without evading possible confrontation. In relation to a curatorial approach, further reflections are necessary in terms of how this contact zone can be extended beyond participative formats or experimental work forms into encounters among artists, as well as between artists and audiences.

In societies characterized by histories of migration, from a transcultural perspective it is also important to attend to labor relations in the respective festivals or institutions, that is, to make sure that these correspond to the respective society's demographic relations as a whole, against the elitist exclusion of minorities.

As event organizers and curators, we often do not fully consider that, like the "white cube," the theater as institution and cultural phenomenon historically presents a European model and is hence fundamentally marked by Eurocentric/Western inscriptions.[3] This also means that the global conditions of theater making are often based on extreme structural and economic discrepancies. As curators, we should reflect further on how to work with locally specific weightings, how to produce even remotely comparable conditions for all invited artists, for instance, by choosing for commissioned works not the stage but a site-specific approach, and so forth.

For the purposes of communication with one's own audiences and for the acquisition of sponsoring and public third-party funding, festivals and programmed series are often given cultural labels that can imply a ghettoization of the artists represented. Rabih Mroué, for instance, has noted on tendencies of being perceived as an ambassador for his country as soon as he leaves Lebanon—to lead the thought to its conclusion, he is ultimately "abused" in his function as artist.[4] For this reason, he avoids taking part

"Show Me The
World," Munich, 2015.
Photo: Stefan Loeber

in "Arabic" programs. This is something that should demonstrate to curators a necessary distancing from what might be called shop windows for nations or continents. This
can mean, for instance, that global themes should be privileged over national questions and, more generally, that the chosen approach should be of similar relevance to all
involved.

We can also frequently observe a paternalistic or maternalistic argument suggest-
ing that productions stemming from non-Western countries appear like plagiarisms and
display too many influences from Western "cultural nations"; consequently, so the argument runs, these are not apt to be shown in the Western metropoles. In this respect,
we can learn from recent research in transcultural art history, research that seeks to
distance itself from a center-periphery logic not by asking about origin and originality
but by concentrating on an analysis of the creativity involved in cultural appropriation.

In turn, it is our task as transculturally active curators to develop strategies of mediation and publicity safeguarding encounters on an equal basis.

This suffices for initial remarks on some of the most important issues; as mentioned, THE DISCUSSION HAS ONLY JUST BEGUN . . .

NOTES

1. The central thesis of the much-discussed exhibition "The Global Contemporary: Art Worlds After 1989" at the Center for Art and Media (ZKM), Karlsruhe (2011–12), was the equation of global and contemporary art after the fall of the wall. Aside from lacking historical perspective, the argumentation was accused especially of a Eurocentric perpetuation of Western standards. See Hans Belting, Andrea Buddensieg, Peter Weibel, eds. *The Global Contemporary and the Rise of the New Art Worlds* (Cambridge, MA : MIT Press, 2013). For a critique of their argument, see Michael Ott, "The Small Aesthetic Difference," Globalismus/Globalism, a special issue of *Texte zur Kunst*, September 2013, 100–109.

2. James Clifford, *Routes, Travel, and Translation in the Late Twentieth Century* (Cambridge, MA: Harvard University Press, 1997).

3. Elena Filipovic, "The Global White Cube," *On-Curating* 22 (2014), http://www.on -curating.org/issue-22-43/the-global-white-cube.html#.WIdPxlMrKUl.

4. Rabih Mroué, "At Least One-Third of the Subject," *Fracija* 55 (2010): 86.

Lygia Clark's *Couple*
(1969) at *Lygia Clark:
The Abandonment of
Art, 1948-1988*, MOMA,
New York, 2014.
Photo: Byron Smith
for the *New York Times*

ANDRÉ LEPECKI

DECOLONIZING THE CURATORIAL

This essay is a very close rendition of a talk I delivered at a 2015 conference in Munich as part of the "Show Me the World" project. It has all the defects and all the advantages of such mode of delivery: it is driven by a kind of circumstantial impetus, in a writing style that has more of the affirmative tone of a manifesto than of paused scholarship. Thus, some concepts (for instance, the aesthetic regime of the arts, *vivência*) and some historical background (the complexities of Lygia Clark's artistic life), even though fully referenced, are not fully explained for the sake of time and focus. For this, I apologize to the reader—I realize those defects in scholarship are perhaps not justifiable in a peer-reviewed journal; however, there is something to be said about the manifesto-like mode of delivery (particularly in the essay's first part) as being in itself the result of careful pondering, to deliver a force, that, in itself, I find to be both theoretically and politically coherent and needed. The essay's title says it all; its goal is not without some high ambitions: to decolonize the curatorial. What remains implicit is that such an act of decolonization has been performed, historically and currently, by very particular objects, actions, and propositions that indeed resist if not subvert altogether the economy circle of *creation → curation → display → perception → valuation → (more or less) creation* that defines the regime of artistic production. In mapping a possible disruption of such economy, as in relating it to a rationality linked, nonmetaphorically, to colonial logic, I feel obliged to write here what I said in Munich as opening remarks before I started reading my paper that fall 2015. What I said then was more or less this:

While preparing my talk, I started to ponder on the two notions that the organizers of the event had asked us all (scholars, artists, programmers, and curators from around the planet) to discuss for three days: "to show," and "the world." I could not help but consider that our gathering on the politics of showing the world would take place in a museum that had been projected by architect Paul Troost under the direct guidance of Adolf Hitler to be the first major display of Nazi ideology and propaganda, a museum that had held the infamous Degenerate Art exhibition of 1937. Haunted by that his-

Theater 47:1   DOI 10.1215/01610775-3710441
© 2017 by André Lepecki

tory, and by the fact that ideologies (whatever they might be) always need to build for themselves their privileged apparatuses of showing their visions of the world, I started to consider what is the exact function of curating in relation to certainly ideological acts of museological "showing" in contemporaneity—given the deeply complex relations between curation (understood as the management of the modes of visibility, valuation, and discursive life of objects, including, but not limited to, art works) and normative-evidentiary politics of presence, particularly in the current context of "the world" we are living in at the moment.

I was also intrigued by that first-person singular pronoun inserted in the event's title, that "me" demanding the world to be shown to him or her and thus turning the title into a very odd imperative. Given all of these factors, in preparing my talk for the conference, I started to think about the notion of curation in relationship to its etymological links to offering cure, to attending, to taking care of. These are always considered positive affects in the practice of curation. But I was also thinking about curating as related to its more recent meaning of being the management of collectible objects, the indexing of archival memories, and the creative implementation of economies of display and of experience economies. In this tension between attending and collecting, a tension of management and economy, of embracing every single object under its very particular mode of intensive care, where the artwork is shown to the

Joseph Goebbels at the exhibition *Degenerate Art*, Haus der Kunst, Berlin, 1938.
Photo courtesy of German Federal Archives

public under the imperative demand of the first-person pronoun *me*, with more or less thick, more or less subtle, but ever-present blanket of meaning and good intentions, it suddenly occurred to me that perhaps what we need at this moment, when the curatorial turn has affirmed itself across the humanities and across all sorts of art forms it had usually been unrelated to, particularly in live performance (dance, theater, performance art, music, sound art, etc., are all now curated, and no longer programmed), that what was interesting to me was to think about artworks and objects that perhaps do not want to be curated: they do not want to be taken care of; they have no need to be taken care of and actually live and thrive and insist on existing without care.

Furthermore, I started to think that the objects and works that usually pose a real political challenge to the situation of the world, to the very logic and irrational reasoning of the functioning of the world, even though coming from artists and their proposals, ontologically resist the curatorial and its apparatuses. And, by doing so, they resist accepting to be captured by normative (even if highly creative and well intended, highly thoughtful and historically grounded) logics of care. Thus, the whole impetus behind

Lygia Clark's
Matchbox Structures
(1964), MOMA,
New York, 2014.
Photo: Byron Smith
for the *New York Times*

this essay is to arrive at those objects that, in their very own materiality and mode of existence as objects, indeed as art objects, remain outside the curatorial, challenging its good intentions and the very stability of the economies of presence and valuation still called "art."

I am interested in objects, practices, propositions, and acts that have nothing to show to a "me" that demands that things must be made visible to perception. I advance that such objects do exist in the world, even in our world, and that they are made by artists and, of course, have much to offer perception and intellection, but mostly they have much to offer to sensation, to affect, to life, to thought, and to a deeper politics. In their singularities, those objects require, demand, offer, open up an altogether different logic for curating. What these objects do, in their integrity and wild living, is to offer to art and to curation decolonizing lines of flight. They are less objects than they are things, thus proposing audiences that are less subjects than things that feel, to use Mario Perniola's expression.[1] Thus the title of this essay, which I will now, (re)begin.

I would like to start by proposing thirteen premises on the conditions that currently condition the making and curating art, and therefore currently condition the situation under which the "world" has to be "shown." These premises are both epistemological clarifications and cartographic assessments. I see them as axiomatic propositions, statements of fact to be placed in space as one distributes vitrines in a gallery. Boring vitrines, made to be passed by without a glance, or smashed with a hammer.

1. The decolonizing movement must be careful in regard to the expression *postcolonial*, since the *post* in *postcolonial* suggests that colonialism is a situation of the past, therefore hiding the current state of a renewed, expanded, and hyperactive colonialist rationality sustaining contemporary political and economic power and their modes of subjectivization.

2. In this sense, even if today, jurisdictionally speaking, the former political formations that linked European nation-states and their colonies in the southern and eastern parts of the globe are no longer in place, the relations between nation-states today (between former colonizing powers, former colonized territories) remain those where the primacy of colonialist logic remains hegemonic, dominant. Moreover, the very logic of biopolitical management and exploitative plundering that characterizes colonialist (non)governance and rationality is now being diverted toward what is still called, for lack of a better word, the Western nation-state.

3. It is impossible to think about the development of capitalism without thinking about the codevelopment of colonialism. One is the other's backside. One is the other's logic in deep correspondence. The many transformations of capitalism over the past centuries (mercantilist capitalism, industrial capitalism, Fordist capitalism, liberal capitalism, neoliberal capitalism, affective capitalism, etc.) are but reflections and inflections of the many transformations endured by colonialism and its modes.

4. The primary principle and first technology binding capitalism and colonialism is that crucial necropolitical invention, the slave, or "the commodity that speaks," to use Fred Moten's expression.[2]

5. Slavery is not only a regime of interpersonal servitude and exploitation (exploitation of labor, of life, of reproductive capacities, of sex, and of desire) but also an entire political technology of subjectivization, one that captures the entire system of conceiving life and its values, life and its agents, life and its objects, and through this capturing transforms all use value into what Michel Serres calls "abuse value."[3]

6. The current metamorphosis of the colonialist-capitalist assemblage has received the name *neoliberalism.* Its most recent effects percolate in the endless wars and more or less carelessly targeted killings taking place in the Middle East under the name of democratic freedom since the inception of neoliberalism in the early 1980s as the hegemonic logic fueling both the rationality and the corporealities of Western power. Here, political scientist Wendy Brown reminds us that neoliberal policies were first implemented in despotic and dictatorial regimes in the 1960s and early 1970s, and that neoliberalism's first steps took place in economic experiments imposed by the International Monetary Fund and World Bank in Western-aligned Latin American and African countries during the 1960s and 1970s, precisely as ways to block real decolonizing or anticapitalist becomings—thus demonstrating how neoliberal necropolitics does not require democracy at all in order to thrive.[4] Think of the economic policies implemented by the infamous "Chicago Boys" in Chile (economists trained at the University of Chicago under Milton Friedman and Arnold Harberger) during Augusto Pinochet's murderous dictatorship in the early 1970s. Think of Margaret Thatcher, one of the major figures behind Western neoliberalism, who until Pinochet's death hosted the former dictator in her own home, calling him a good friend and honorable man, to whom "Britain was greatly indebted."[5]

7. It is impossible to delink neoliberal "political economy" and its "distinct mode of reason, of the production of subjects, of 'conduct of conduct', and as a scheme of valuation,"[6] from the increased phenomena of endemic warfare in the Middle East; from the rise of concentration camps in the West (whether these camps are for migrants and refugees displaced by the most recent colonial adventures that have shaped Euro-American policies for centuries, or for that new legal category for bare life, the "enemy combatant"); from the legal assassinations of Western citizens by their own governments thanks to executive fiat or secret presidential orders; or from the overwhelming surveillance of the very citizens of the enlightened, reasonable, and free West. This endemic logic of always rationalized and always "reasonable" brutality for the sake of security reminds us (as Paul Gilroy has, in his book *Postcolonial Melancholia*) that the colony (and not the camp, as Giorgio Agamben posits) is indeed the *nomos* of neoliberal Western democracy.[7]

8. So, if this is the scenario, if this is the situation conditioning the conditions of existence, of living life, experiencing death, making love, creating art, curating exhibitions, consuming, and participating, then what does it mean to decolonize? It means to affirm a logic of living and a desire for collective sociability that are altogether different in their ways of establishing relations between subjects, between objects and subjects, between matters and subjects, between matters and matters, between human animals and nonhuman animals, between life and death, life and art, death and art, in order to bring about other logics of existence—modes of existence as the insistence to openly fight against what Katherine McKittrick and Sylvia Wynter have called "the imperial and colonial liberal monohumanist premises" of existence.[8]

Lygia Clark's *Water and Seashells* (1970), MOMA, New York, 2014. Photo: Byron Smith for the *New York Times*

9. In this struggle, could something like art and something like curating still be the answers for all of these challenges, for all of these questions that the world, our world, our contemporaneity, pretty much everywhere, throws at us, particularly given the fact that this reality, this situation, is also being made by us, even at the moment when we sit here, maybe even because we are at this moment sitting here? Moreover, could something like live art (dance, performance, body art, theater, music) and the curation of live art be the answer, have the answer, or at least build or name or enact some weapons to fight the situation? If we decide to answer these questions affirmatively, then how does a curator cowork, or coimagine, or colabor along with the works and artists putting their bodies (and bodies of work) on the line, to precipitate the advent of another logic of relation between live art objects and their publics?

10. In a recent essay, which I am still trying to figure out whether I read correctly, Maurizio Lazzarato, commenting on Jacques Rancière's notion of the "aesthetic regime of the arts" (which is the only one, if you remember Rancière's tripartition of artistic regimes, where art and politics share one common element which is dissensus), states bluntly: "The aesthetic regime of the arts—precisely where we no longer are."[9] As I said, I am not totally sure of what Lazzarato actually means by this short affirmation, but I will agree with the sentence nevertheless, or use this sentence nevertheless, to say that, indeed, this concept or understanding of the relations between art and politics is indeed totally insufficient to respond to, account for, and go against the premises of "the imperial and colonial liberal monohumanism" of our times, to invoke once again McKittrick and Wynter.[10] I am taking here the liberty to overread, and perhaps even misread, what Lazzarato might have wanted to say with his sentence. I am over- or misreading him to say that, yes, to make an art object so that it merely redistributes the senses, so that it troubles the relation between what is sayable and what is visible (first about what is artistically given to view, and hopefully later on to the social sphere) is clearly no longer enough in our situation.[11] Why? Because the system of objects within the aesthetic regime of the arts remains entrapped, encased, imprisoned by, and subjected to the general system of colonialist subjectivization, of course, neoliberal style, that is, filled with little freedoms and exciting pornopharmacological fluxes, surprising rearrangements around sense and sense, but still living in the generalized field of meaning and rationality conditioning the conditions of liberal, colonial monohumanism. And, if the system of objects remains the same, it follows that the system of subjects remains entrapped in the same logic of mutual copossession, since, as Moten reminds us, "while subjectivity is defined by the subject's possession of itself and its objects, it is troubled by a dispossessive force objects exert such that the subject seems to be possessed—infused, deformed—by the object it possesses."[12] This dynamic is what keeps the aesthetic object (even a live one) in its proper place. Because this is what an object does, according to the American philosopher of ethics Silvia Benso, in her book *The Face of Things*: an object is "an endless reproduction and confirmation of the manipulative abilities of the subject."[13]

11. So what is the style of neoliberal imperial colonialism that both manipulates and is manipulated by contemporary hegemonic monohumanism and its aesthetic objects? It is the style that finds in the reinforcement of identity as representation a way to perform unquestioned institutional good intentions. In other words, under institutional goodwill the quiet reification of colonialist identity politics becomes one of the major ways that curation, as an art of neoliberal inclusion, is set to work. It works not to promote any radical or antinormative potentialities in the works presented, not for the sake of the potentiality and radical alternatives for living and existing performed by works and artists; rather, institutional good intentions perform that essential task for the colonialist rationality: to demonstrate and perform a certain image of inclusive democratic goodwill in the art houses of the ever well-meaning and yet relentlessly racist Western centers of power.

12. So, to decolonize curatorial imagination is to end the ways systems of objects and subjects (even after the official end of colonialism as a political regime) keep colonialist logic in place. We can invoke here Jack Halberstam explaining how Moten understands Frantz Fanon as "wanting 'not the end of colonialism'—or not just the end of colonialism—'but the end of the standpoint from which colonialism makes sense.'"[14] And what would not make sense from the standpoint of curatorial logic? To replace objects by *things*. Once again, Silvia Benso is helpful: "Only if things are recognized in their own peculiar alterity which does not submit, because it cannot be submissible, to the categories of the subject, can any ecological project" (and here the ecological stands for a planetary ethical-political project absolutely outside of the logic that make exploitative colonial-capitalism possible) "be grounded on something more profound and fundamental than the fortuitous occurrence of subjects of good will."[15]

13. In this sense, beyond the occasional and fortuitous goodwill of subjects curating and presenting objects as identitary proxies, and performances of immunized inclusion, we need another logic of curation, decolonized even from the accepted gestures of what it means to be a progressive subject. In this new alogical mode of curating, instead of objects (including performances) and experiences (of performances) we would have instead *things* and *vivências* (the term used by Lygia Clark and Hélio Oiticica to describe the lived experience of experimentation, always linked to both action and speech, the forces of matter and the forces of desire), regarding which neither capitalism and colonialism, and even less neoliberal subjectivity, has any patience for and no desire whatsoever to assimilate. Against all the common assumptions that whatever exists in the world not only might but certainly will be assimilated, colonized, and turned into profit by capitalism, the living experience of the subaltern nevertheless shows us that there are a few *things* that capitalism, neoliberal subjectivity, and colonialist rapacity cannot and will not digest. What? Who? Stefano Harney and Moten answer point blank: "The fat ones. The ones who are out of all compass however precisely they are located."[16]

Out of compass, out of time, time to invoke now one particularly powerful mode of existence of this excess; an artist and her things whose existence out of compass exactly, rigorously, beautifully, advanced the promise of a decolonized art.

Lygia Clark's *Bichos* (1959-1966), MOMA, New York, 2014. Photo: Byron Smith for the *New York Times*

It is well known the extreme difficulty of presenting in museums and other more or less well-defined art contexts (biennials, galleries) the series of works that Lygia Clark started to make from 1964 onward, particularly once Clark started insisting on what she called "propositions": participatory works where "the act" was the work itself. One of the main difficulties derives from the fact that Clark's acts do not at all belong to the "experience economy" that also founds neoliberal logic. Rather, as Clark insisted with increased emphasis, the act had to be understood in its most *immanent* dimension. Thus, acts had to be carried out without an audience, without institutional framing marking them as art, and without any object to serve as proof that an art project had taken place. In other words, there would be nothing to be exhibited.

For Clark, there was no difference between the exhibition of art objects and the self-exhibition of subjects experimenting with art—thus her extreme dislike of the genres of body art and performance art, in relation to which she vehemently refused to belong, since she saw these new genres emerging alongside her own artistic trajectory from the 1950s to the 1970s as operating an even more perverse colonization: the artist replaces the object and becomes now the sole object of praise. Exhibiting was precisely what had to be troubled to the very core, since it is predicated on a coformation object-subject that kept their stable relations in place, regardless of the novelty of that relation. Clark's challenge to the economy of curatorial imagination was beginning. It would reach its apex in the late 1970s and in the 1980s with her relational objects and her therapy practice known as "structuring of the self" on the application of precarious, paradoxical objects[17]—made of plastic bags filled with air or water, shells, pantyhose holding rocks or Ping-Pong balls, a loofah, a flashlight, plastic tubes into which Clark would blow air or make soft noises, small cloth bags filled with sand, and many others—on naked bodies of her patients.

I am interested in the persistence of the essential difficulty of showing or displaying or curating Clark's relational objects. It is a difficulty that is constantly being reiterated by the most well-informed, well-intentioned, careful and caring curators and institutions, including the most open, experimental, and knowledgeable curators working on Clark's ideas. And yet, the persistence of Clark's sensorial and relational works as a *difficult thing*, the status of the relational objects as difficult things to curate, reveal

that what these works do is not simply to pose yet another difficult intellectual and perceptual challenge to a curator's creativity—like an interesting problem that needs to find its proper (albeit difficult) solution. Rather, the difficulty in curating these works derives from the very fact of their aesthetic singularity; it derives from their *thingness*, their existence in active exteriority to, and radical escape from, regimes of display that subjugate and colonize the relational objects as being Clark's objects and the participants as being the new authors/artists of a Lygia Clark work. Clark's works are difficult exactly because (and to invoke again Moten's quote on the unassimilable ontology and constitutive fugitivity of things) they "are out of all compass however precisely they are located." Thus, we must take seriously the diagnosis made by Suely Rolnik, Brazilian art and cultural critic and Lygia Clark specialist, when she wrote:

> Taken back to the display case, and therefore to the pedestal, their freedom to live unattached in the world, to benefit from affective intimacy with the largest possible number and variety of others, was pruned away. For this reason, the first part of the artist's work (from 1948 to 1963) is the best known, with the *Bichos* at its apogee, perhaps because they were the last of Clark's objects *capable of being neutralized by the art system* and of being consumed as simple, inoffensive objects of art, with their value determined solely by the market. Until the end of the artist's life (and even many years after her death), her works from this period, specially the *Bichos*, would

be the ones privileged in countless one-person or group exhibitions and would by the same token constitute the focus of the majority of the studies of her work.[18]

Privileging the *Bichos* and not knowing what to do with the relational and sensorial objects is exactly what took place in the recent and otherwise absolutely excellent and indeed superbly curated exhibition *Lygia Clark: The Abandonment of Art* at MOMA in 2014. Curated by Connie Butler and Luis Pérez-Oramas, the exhibition was the first major retrospective of Clark's oeuvre in the United States. It was preceded by at least three years of intense consultation seminars, both in Brazil and in the United States, in which Butler and Pérez-Oramas conducted several high-intensity meetings not only with Clark scholars, collectors, curators but also with visual artists, performance artists, poets, and musicians that either had a history of working with or around Clark or felt they belonged to a kind of heritage of Clark.

I had the good fortune of being invited by the two curators to participate in some of the meetings, as well as to write an essay on Lygia Clark's relation to performance for the exhibition catalog.[19] In the meetings, Butler's and Pérez-Oramas's deep knowledge, understanding, concern regarding the integrity of Clark's oeuvre, and openness to different opinions and critiques were exemplary. They invariably asked participants to offer ideas on how to approach those particularly difficult things—the infamous relational objects, which Clark had created totally outside of any concerns that characterize the "aesthetic regime of the arts" altogether. And collectively, the conclusion was always the same: these are impossible objects for the museum. Their existence takes place outside of curatorial care.

Why are Clark's relational objects so difficult? Because the problem posed by these objects to the art system at large requires a fundamental decolonization. Their nature is indeed essentially offensive to the very gesture of curating them. They remain wild in their singularity. This is derived from the fact that the relational objects are precisely and essentially *nonobjects*—to use the concept Brazilian critic Ferreira Gullar had already used in his 1959 prescient essay on Clark's relentless logic of approaching the object, identifying the demise of objecthood from Clark's works decades before this expulsion's apex, the object's exodus from the realm of the curatorial, in the 1980s.[20]

Now, if the relational objects are indeed nonobjects, it follows that their existence proposes the formation of nonsubjects. Indeed, here lies the absolute resistance of these singular matters and assemblages to "being neutralized by the system of art," as Rolnik writes.[21] Their resistance, their objection, their offensive against art economies and intensive cares express not a failure in curatorial imagination in finding "the right solution" for the exhibition of the relational objects in exhibition contexts but the sheer insistence of their ontopolitical force *as* nonobjects, their *thingness*—their *wild* thingness. Clark's relational objects do "tel[l] us that there is a wild beyond to the structures we inhabit and that inhabit us," to invoke once again Halberstam's comments on the wild thing.[22]

The relational objects initiate an altogether different logic for objects and subjects to insist in, exist in, the situation that is violently inhospitable to their existence; theirs is a logic that escapes not just the art system but the whole system of subjectivity predicated on the authorial/manipulating subject and the authored/manipulable object that confirms the author's upper hand, controlling and commanding. Clark's nonobjects effectively neutralize and even demolish the very premises of the art system: they cannot be digested by it, as much as the art system tries to incorporate them, swallow them, bring them into good care. Why? Because these nonobjects and their related experiences as *vivência* are ontopolitically offensive to the very premises of curatorial reason.

Why do I use such a word, *offensive*? Because it is a word that surfaces on the lips of an art critic emerging from the depths of experiencing those objects on his body, after a session with Clark, as documented in *Memória do Corpo*, a film made a few months before Clark's death in her small apartment in Copacabana, where Clark had been conducting her therapy sessions since early 1980, by using several of her odd nonobjects on her many patients. Shot in 1984, the thirty-one-minute-long video by Brazilian film director Mário Carneiro documents Clark's uses of the relational objects in her practice she called "structuring of the self" (the video was premiered at Galeria Paulo Klabin in Rio de Janeiro in that same year). For the purposes of documentation, Clark's "patient" was the Brazilian art critic Paulo Sérgio Duarte.

I would like to concentrate on one striking moment when Duarte is starting to come out of the long therapy session, in which the patient eventually lies covered by the very peculiar and paradoxical relational objects on a large and very soft bed, and begins to share with Clark his *vivência*—that is, starts to verbalize the sensations he had throughout the session, what Clark called the expression of the "phantasmatics." After commenting on the effects of a drop of honey Clark had inserted between his lips sometime during the session, Duarte, a man whose extreme care with words made his fame as an art critic, continues to describe his experience with the relational objects. He starts a sentence but stops right after pronouncing just the first word; he pauses, ponders, eyes still shut while lying almost totally naked on the large bed. His pause takes a few long seconds, and finally he says: "Eu não sei se ofende a eles chamar eles de 'coisa,' mas todas as vezes que eles estão passando em cima de mim eu era sobretudo pele, sobretudo superfície. Muito bom isso." (I don't know if it offends them to call them "things," but every time that they are passing over me I was [*sic*] above all skin, above all surface. That's very good.)

"I don't know if it offends them to call them 'things.'" It is this critical declension of Clark's famous *relational objects* (the way the objects are known, cataloged) into *things*, performed by the art critic, carefully, cautiously, that I find absolutely crucial. His words

are totally accurate. The polite hesitation showed by Duarte in pondering whether by calling the objects *things* he was offending them actually reveals the aggregating and fugitive simultaneous double-decolonizing movement operated by things. If Duarte is polite, the thing's move away from its objecthood is not polite at all: it is actually an offensive offense of things against a whole system of rationalized curatorial and art-historical inscriptions, since it is precisely thanks to their paradoxical motions away from objecthood, and therefore away from affirming subjecthood, that things stop serving both subjectivity *and* objectivity and advance another kind of relational potentiality, a new understanding of life totally away from the daily repertoire of predetermined actions, desires, thoughts, and habitus.

The reconcretion of the work of art as the work of thingly fugitivity toward a more potent living, a move that Clark had already announced as early as 1956 in a lecture at the Escola de Arquitetura of the Federal University of Minas Gerais in her native city of Belo Horizonte (two years before Allan Kaprow announced a "new concrete art" in which "all of life" would be at hand as material), required a double dissolution, a double becoming imperceptible: "The work of art once again takes on the sense of anonymity" and "the artist thus abdicates something of his personality," as Clark wrote in her 1965 text (published for the first time in 1982–83), "On the Magic of the Object."[23] Here, we find ourselves before a radically different vision of art, in which what is at stake is not Kaprow's blurring of art and life, to use Jeff Kelley's famous expression on Kaprow's work,[24] but a total dissolution of the central figure that creates the binary: the artist as exceptional object of praise.

The artwork's thingliness accompanies an antiepideictic understanding of the artist's presence and subjectivity, but this understanding must also be extended to the participant, in what Annette Leddy (in a different context) called a "person-eliminative approach" to art.[25] Anticipating Roberto Esposito's insight that "the person is not to be conceived of as the only form within which life is destined to flow,"[26] Clark both theorized and practiced a positive understanding of the impersonal against "a romantic attitude by the artist who still needs an object, *even if he is the object*, in order to deny it" as she writes so clearly in the early 1970s.[27]

The unassimilable thing's force, its offense to a whole art system, which is also a whole system of subjectivity, finds its ultimate expression in the curious option not to show the iconic and rarely seen film *Memória do Corpo* in the MOMA exhibition (it had been shown, for instance, in Catherine David's 1997 *documentaX*). The absence of this important film in an exhibition that tried so hard to include the experiential-participatory dimension of Clark's work (and, moreover, the film that would indicate clearly to the MOMA public what the "abandonment of art" that titled the MOMA exhibition actually meant for Clark—the abandonment of a whole logic of existence that keeps in place the violent colonizations of body and thought precisely as long as art exists under the regime of the object-subject relation) already indicates the problems that the thing, the *offensive* thing, the always fugitive thing poses to curating. I believe it is not only that the relational objects are indeed wild things. In being wild things, they recast Clark's subjectivity itself, casting her into the side of noncuratable artists as well. Clark is then also a nonsubject, thanks to her daring, to her integrity, to her refusal to participate in a whole logic that still keeps in place the situation that makes our world showable to an endlessly demanding "me, me, me, me." Her position is transparently clear in the film. Her firm logic is as wild as the relational objects she holds, caresses, puts on her body, puts on Duarte's body, gives voice to. In that, Clark partakes of the nature of things. Neither posthuman nor neohuman, neither parahuman nor prehuman, the *offense of things* names an act of insubordinate interanimation, revealing what is always underlying those dyads: an ongoing revolt against the colonizing entrapments of subjectivity and objectivity, the organic and the inorganic, art and life.

NOTES

1. Mario Perniola, *The Sex Appeal of the Inorganic* (New York: Continuum, 2004).

2. Fred Moten, *In the Break: The Aesthetics of the Black Radical Tradition* (Minneapolis: University of Minnesota Press, 2003); Stefano Harney and Fred Moten, *The Undercommons: Fugitive Planning and Black Study* (New York: Minor Compositions, 2013).

3. Michel Serres and Lawrence R. Schehr, *The Parasite* (Minneapolis: University of Minnesota Press, 2007), 80.

4. Wendy Brown, *Undoing the Demos: Neoliberalism's Stealth Revolution* (Cambridge, MA: Zone, 2015).

5. For an account see "Thatcher Stands by Pinochet," BBC News, 1999 : http://news .bbc.co.uk/2/hi/304516.stm. Robin Harris, former member of Thatcher's policy team, also defended Thatcher's "respect" and sense of "debt" to Pinochet: "[Thatcher] also took a positive view of Pinochet's 17 years in power. There was certainly great violence. But the loss of life, most of which occurred in the first months when a civil war raged, was less than in other similar situations." Harris concludes his article for *The Telegraph* with these astonishing words: "Margaret Thatcher has nothing to be ashamed of in defending Augusto Pinochet, when others refused to do so. But he was lucky to find such *a champion.*" (Robin Harris, "Thatcher Always Honoured Britain's Debt to Pinochet," *The Telegraph*, December 13, 2006, http://www.telegraph. co.uk/comment/personal -view/3635244/Thatcher-always-honoured-Britains-debt-to-Pinochet.html.)

6. Ibid.

7. Paul Gilroy, *Postcolonial Melancholia* (New York: Columbia University Press, 2006). Giorgio Agamben, *Homo sacer: sovereign power and bare life* (Stanford: Stanford University Press, 1998).

8. Katherine McKittrick, *Sylvia Wynter: On Being Human as Praxis* (Durham, NC: Duke University Press, 2015), 13.

9. Maurizio Lazzarato, "Art, Work, and Politics in Disciplinary Societies and Societies of Security," in *Spheres of Action: Art and Politics*, ed. Éric Alliez and Peter Osborne

(Cambridge, MA: MIT Press, 2011), 42. For Rancière's views on the relation between aesthetics and politics predicted not their shared dissensus, see: Jacques Rancière, "Ten Theses on Politics," in *Dissensus: On Politics and Aesthetics* (New York: Continuum Press; 2010) and Jacques Rancière, *The Politics of Aesthetics. The Distribution of the Sensible.* (New York: Continuum Press, 2004).

10. McKittrick, *Sylvia Wynter*, 13.

11. Lazzarato, "Art, Work, and Politics," 42.

12. Moten, *In the Break*, 1.

13. Silvia Benso, *The Face of Things: A Different Side of Ethics* (Albany, NY: State University of New York Press, 2000), xxxiii.

14. Jack Halberstam, quoted in Harney and Moten, *Undercommons*, 8.

15. Benso, *Face of Things*, xx.

16. Harney and Moten, *Undercommons*, 52.

17. On Clark's work as paradoxical practice, see Eleonora Fabião, "The Making of a Body: Lygia Clark's *Anthropophagic Slobber*," in *Lygia Clark,* ed. Connie Butler and Luis Peres-Oramas (New York: Museum of Modern Art, 2014).

18. Suely Rolnik, "Molding a Contemporary Soul: The Empty-Full of Lygia Clark," in *The Experimental Exercise of Freedom*, ed. Rina Carvajal (Los Angeles: Museum of Contemporary Art, 2000), 73–74; emphasis added.

19. Once the exhibition opened, Eleonora Fabião (who also participated in one meeting held by Pérez-Oramas and Butler in Rio de Janeiro, and was also invited by them to contribute as well with an essay to the MOMA catalog) and I were invited to coteach a workshop on Lygia Clark's participatory approach to art at MOMA's education department.

20. Ferreira Gullar [1959], "Teoria do Não-objeto," in *Experiência Neoconcreta* (São Paulo: Cosac Naify, 2007), 90–94.

21. Suely Rolnik, "Molding a Contemporary Soul: The Empty-Full of Lygia Clark," in *The Experimental Exercise of Freedom*, ed. Rina Carvajal (Los Angeles: Museum of Contemporary Art, 2000).

22. Halberstam, quoted in Harney and Moten, *Undercommons*, 7.

23. Lygia Clark, "On the Magic of the Object," *Lygia Clark* exhibition catalogue (Barcelona: Fundacion Tápies, 1998 [1965]), 152–54.

24. Even though I was never able to find a text by Kaprow where he uses this exact formulation, a very close one can be found in his 1966 book *Assemblages, Environments, and Happenings*: "The dividing line between art and life should remain as fluid and indistinct as possible." See Allan Kaprow, *Assemblage, Environments, and Happenings* (New York: H. N. Abrams, 1966), 190. See also Allan Kaprow and Jeff Kelley, *Essays on the Blurring of Art and Life: Allan Kaprow*, ed. Jeff Kelley (Berkeley: University of California Press, 2003).

25. Annette Leddy, "Intimate: The Allan Kaprow Papers," in *Allan Kaprow: Art as Life*, ed. Eva Meyer-Hermann, Andrew Perchuk, and Stephanie Rosenthal (Los Angeles: Getty Publications, 2008), 43.

26. Roberto Esposito, *The Third Person (*New York: Polity Books, 2011) 140.

27. Lygia Clark, "On the Suppression of the Object (notes)," *Lygia Clark* exhibition catalogue (Barcelona: Fundacion Tápies, 1998 [1975]), 265.

Suely Rolnik

Translated by Pablo Lafuente and Vivian Mocellin

The Knowing-Body Compass
in Curatorial Practices

"Integrated world capitalism": Capitalism is worldwide and integrated, because it has potentially colonized the whole of the planet, because it currently lives in symbiosis with countries that seemed to have escaped from it (such as those from the Soviet Bloc, China) and because it tends to ensure that no human activity, no production sector, escapes its control.
—Félix Guattari, 1980[1]

We address the unconscious who protest. We are looking for allies. We need allies. We have the impression that our allies are already there, that they are ahead of us, that there are a lot of people who have had enough, who think, feel, and work in a direction analogous to ours: it is not a fashion but something deeper, a spirit of the times, in which convergent investigations have been developed, in very different domains.
—Gilles Deleuze and Félix Guattari, "Sur Capitalisme et Schizophrénie," 1972[2]

Before beginning this article, I must say that I'm not familiar with the specific questions that curatorial practices raise in the field of theater and performance. So I'll problematize the figure of the curator as I know it in the visual arts, where it appeared first, hoping to offer some tools to think about it outside of this particular terrain.

The Figure of the Curator and Its Genealogy

The role of conceiving and organizing public exhibitions of artworks originates, together with such exhibitions, in the eighteenth century, and, like the artworks, it acquired an increasing importance throughout the nineteenth and twentieth centuries. However, the figure of the curator under such a name and as we know it today—its proliferation worldwide and its seductive power over the new generations, which goes together with the multiplication of curatorial schools everywhere—emerged in the context of the consolidation of the power of worldwide financialized capitalism, from the mid-1970s on.[3] Because the main source of energy of the new regime is the force of creation chan-

Theater 47:1 DOI 10.1215/01610775-3710465
© 2017 by Suely Rolnik

neled into the force of creativity, it directly affects the field of art in many ways. One of them is the need for a constant negotiation among the artist, the institution where his/her work will be exhibited, and the investors (collectors, galleries, sponsors, etc.)—with the latter tending to have more and more power, as all human activities tend to be financialized in the new regime, especially those that can feed its need for "novelties," preferably with strength of seduction as is often the case in the practice of art.

The curator is the mediator in the dispute between the distinct interests in that triangle. The curator's position depends on the destiny of this dispute and the kind of curatorial action that will be undertaken. From a micropolitical point of view, what distinguishes those positions is, on the one hand, the degree of each curator's vulnerability to art, as well as the type of value the curator attributes to it, and on the other, the curator's degree of identification with the world of those who invest capital in art. These two factors will define where the curator establishes the boundary between the negotiable and the nonnegotiable. The difference between those perspectives is not neutral: they implicate distinct criteria according to which the curators will choose the artworks to be shown, the ways they will be presented and related to one another, and their effects on the subjectivity of the publics and, therefore, in the social field.

My focus here is on two fictitious types of curator that occupy the opposite extremes of the vast, diverse, and complex range of perspectives of curatorial practices. Such fiction is a way to picture the divergent vectors of forces at stake in this field. The kind of politics of desire that guides each of those two types in their performances will allow me to point out the distinction between them. To do so, I will first invoke two concepts on which I have been working for the last few years: the *colonial-capitalistic unconscious* and the *knowing-body*.

The Colonial-Capitalistic Unconscious: Obstructing the Knowing-Body

I call *colonial-capitalistic* the dominant regime of the unconscious in modern Western culture. If I chose those two words to name it and link them by a dash, it is because the origin of capitalism is inseparable from the colonizing enterprise of large parts of the planet, carried out by western Europe since the end of fourteenth and the beginning of fifteenth century. But it is also—and most of all—because after different unfoldings of this regime during the last five centuries, in its contemporary version it has expanded its colonial project to the world at large, to the point that we can refer to it as *integrated world capitalism*, as Félix Guattari proposed in 1980, when the new dynamic and characteristics of capitalism were barely establishing themselves.[4] Because it is in this frame that the figure of the curator emerged, it is important to focus on the predominant politics of the unconscious in the new regime, in order to problematize what would tell both fictional perspectives apart.

The colonial-capitalistic unconscious is the micropolitical dynamic of this regime. The fact that it is its invisible dimension does not make it less real in its presence and effects. It gives the regime its existential consistency, without which it would not be able to maintain itself. It is a certain way of producing subjectivity and desire predominant in societies under integrated world capitalism—that is to say, predominant within ourselves. Such unconscious is characterized by the obstruction of the knowing-body.

To situate what I mean by *knowing-body*, I invoke Lygia Clark, a Brazilian artist who invented especially refined dispositives to shift out from the colonial-capitalistic unconscious. I focus on her proposition *Caminhando (Walking)*.

WALKING ALONG THE MÖBIUS STRIP WITH LYGIA CLARK

The origin of *Caminhando* was a study Clark made in 1963 for a work that opened a new phase of her *Bichos* series. The new direction of her investigation consisted in exploring the Möbius strip, a strip of just one surface in which the edge of one of its sides continues on the reverse of the other side, which makes them indistinguishable and creates a topological surface.

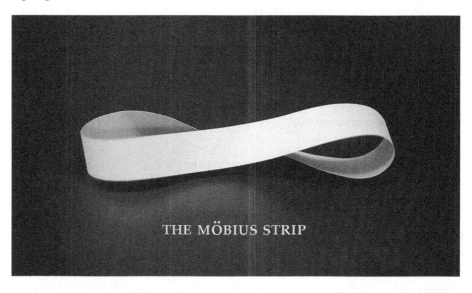

THE MÖBIUS STRIP

Sequential images:
Rodrigo Araujo

In her study for this new phase of her *Bichos*, Clark explored longitudinal cuts in a Möbius strip made of paper. In this process the artist noticed that it is in the actual moment of cutting that the work came into existence. More precisely, it became clear for her that the work itself *is* this action and the experience that it gives rise to, and not the object that results from it. It consists in the opening to a new way of seeing and feeling time and space—a time without before and after, and a space without inside and outside, above and below, front and reverse, left and right. It is the discovery of a time immanent to the act of cutting: the becoming of the strip that takes place at each turn of the cutting of its surface. In this experience, the space is not a separate entity from the strip's surface, and it cannot be dissociated from time: there is a becoming of its shapes along with the becoming of the strip surface through the acts of cutting.

This revelation perplexed Clark and led her to transform the experience into an artistic proposition that she named *Caminhando*. It consists of offering the public strips of paper, scissors, and glue, together with very simple instructions. Whoever is willing to live this work must take ownership of those objects and follow Clark's instructions: they must twist the paper strip and glue onto one of its ends the reverse side of the other end, creating their own Möbius strip. Then they should choose any point of the surface to begin cutting from there, along its surface, with just one warning: to avoid the points that had already being chosen to cut in each turn. The act of cutting must go on until the surface is exhausted and there is no more space to make a new cut. In this moment, whether or not they respect the artist's warning, the strip will be once more a surface with two sides, with front and reverse, inside and outside, above and below, left and right. It will no longer be a topological surface.

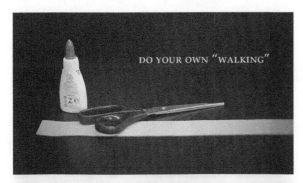

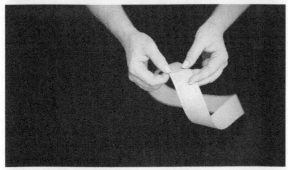

The warning is, certainly, not a mere artist's whim; on the contrary, the very possibility of the work itself depends on following it, because the act of cutting is not neutral: its effects vary depending on the type of cutting that each person makes in his or her "walking." If we pay attention to her warning and choose a new point to continue the cutting each time that the point chosen earlier is met, a difference will be produced on the surface's shape and on the space that is created with it by each turn of the act of cutting. The shapes of surface and space will be multiplied in a continuous variation that is exhausted only when there is no more surface to cut. The work is made through the repetition of the act that opens this other kind of space and time experience. In other words, the work itself is this event, which materializes in the differences introduced in the strip's surface and, inextricably, in subjectivity's experience—their becoming others.

IF YOU AVOID THE SAME
POINTS TO CONTINUE CUTTING

YOUR ACTIONS
PRODUCE DIFFERENCES

If, in contrast, Clark's instructions are not followed, and we insist on cutting through the same point at each turn, the result is an infinite reproduction of the initial shape. This form repeats itself, identically, each time the action is repeated, until there is no more surface to cut. This type of cutting is a sterile act: there is no artwork. More precisely, there is no event in which the work as such would be accomplished. The absence of an event manifests in the fact that no difference is created in the strip's surface.

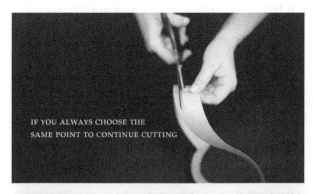

IF YOU ALWAYS CHOOSE THE
SAME POINT TO CONTINUE CUTTING

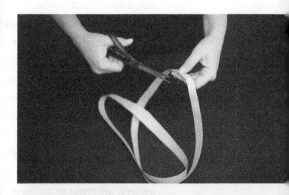

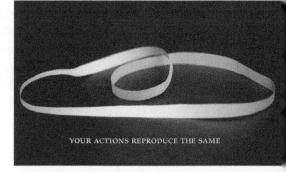

YOUR ACTIONS REPRODUCE THE SAME

But what does the uniqueness of this experience consists of? What gives it the status of an event? To answer these questions, first I need to present some relatively dense ideas that will take some of the reader's time. They concern two of the multiple simultaneous experiences we have of the world, each resulting from different capacities that subjectivity has to apprehend it. The definition of a politics of desire—and, therefore, a regime of the unconscious—depends on the degree to which the subjectivity uses, or does not use, these capacities. If I need to take this detour it is because it will provide us with a magnifying lens to see in detail the distinct vectors at stake in curatorial practices, by means of the politics of desire that prevails in each of them.

The World, Each World, Is a Möbius Strip

Let's imagine that the world—or, rather, each world—is a Möbius strip. One of the sides of the strip that gives rise to its Möbius structure would be the form of a world, in its concrete exteriority, which we refer to as reality; and the other, the forces that agitate it in its condition as a living body. They constitute one and a unique face of the world's topological-relational surface, made of all kinds of bodies—human and nonhuman—in varied and variable connections and disconnections. Thus, forces and forms are inextricably linked, as the force of life is unlimited and doesn't exist without its provisional materialization in different kinds of bodies, which are finite.

The signs of the forces and forms are registered through two different capacities in our *sensory* organs, as they are called in Western culture. Those capacities act simultaneously and are inextricably linked, as forms and forces are inseparable in the topological-relational surface of a world. They are at work independently of whether or not, and to what extent, we are aware of them and manage to keep them active in our evaluations to guide our choices and our actions.

The apprehension of the forms of the bodies and their relations are made through perception (sensorial experience) and feelings (the experience of psychological emotion). Such experiences, provided by the those organs in their sensorial corporality, are articulated according to the existing social-cultural codes, which delimit places that we are identified with, their distribution in the society, inseparable of the distribution of the access to goods and of wealth, their hierarchies of power and their representations. We project onto the forms we perceive the representations we associate to them, to assign them meaning. Thus, these codes function as a guide to locate ourselves in society, allowing us to decipher its forms and dynamics. In other words, such capacity corresponds to a cognitive apprehension of the world, a rational knowledge that fulfills the functions of socialization and communication, necessary for us to exist within a social and historical environment. It is subjectivity's experience as a subject, which I qualify as personal-sensorial-psychological, structured by social-cultural codes. It is an experience of the world in its actual state, which is familiar to us because it is marked by the cultural habits that format us and drive us in daily life, by means of recognition.

In Western and Westernized societies—which under integrated world capitalism tend to encompass the whole planet—the familiarity with this capacity is reinforced and amplified by the fact that we tend to be restricted to it within the dominant politics of subjectivation in those societies. Such reduction of subjectivity to its experience as a subject and of the world to its objectivity is one of the fundamental aspects of the colonial-capitalistic unconscious.

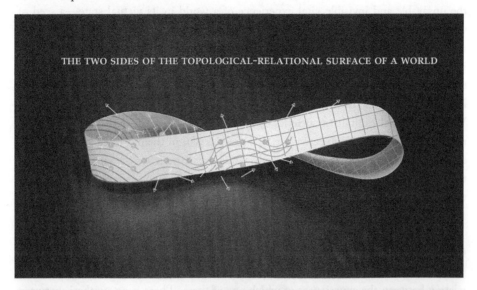

THE TWO SIDES OF THE TOPOLOGICAL-RELATIONAL SURFACE OF A WORLD

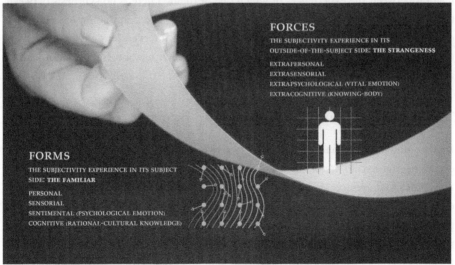

FORCES
THE SUBJECTIVITY EXPERIENCE IN ITS
OUTSIDE-OF-THE-SUBJECT SIDE: **THE STRANGENESS**

EXTRAPERSONAL
EXTRASENSORIAL
EXTRAPSYCHOLOGICAL (VITAL EMOTION)
EXTRACOGNITIVE (KNOWING-BODY)

FORMS
THE SUBJECTIVITY EXPERIENCE IN ITS SUBJECT
SIDE: **THE FAMILIAR**

PERSONAL
SENSORIAL
SENTIMENTAL (PSYCHOLOGICAL EMOTION)
COGNITIVE (RATIONAL-CULTURAL KNOWLEDGE)

The experience of the forces that agitate reality is the result of another capacity from those same organs, the extrasensorial one: the capacity for being affected by these forces, which is made possible by their resonating-relational corporality, a feature that belongs to our condition as living beings. Those effects present themselves by means of percepts (the extrasensorial experience) and affects (the experience of vital emotions in their different degrees of strength). They are new ways of seeing and feeling that don't carry with them words, images, or gestures. They provide subjectivity with extracognitive power to evaluate its environment, an etho-ecological apprehension that I call the *knowing-body*. It is the outside-of-the-subject experience of subjectivity, the unsayable and invisible vital experience of a world in its virtual state—a seed of world composed by those percepts and affects that pulsate in all the bodies belonging to the same environment. They are the singular resonances of the common field of forces inhabiting each of them, shared by empathy. I qualify this experience as extrapersonal-extrasensorial-extrapsychological (vital emotion). It is an atmosphere that overflows lived situations and throws us into a state of strangeness. This state is intensified in Western colonial-capitalistic societies by the tendency to be dissociated from this experience in the politics of subjectivation that prevails within them. Pulled apart from the experience these fluxes effect on our body, we cannot experience the virtual worlds that those effects carry with them. This is why we call those organs *sensory organs*, ignoring their extrasensorial capacity. The obstruction of the knowing-body is another essential aspect of the colonial-capitalistic unconscious.

As forces and forms inseparably constitute a one-faced topological-relational surface and, at the same time, function according to different logics, scales, and velocities, the dynamic between them is not of opposition but of a paradox, as it is paradoxical the relation between the experiences of which one of them. There is no synthesis between those two different experiences (not even dialectics), or the domination of one by the other in an alleged process of cognitive development, or even less any possibility of achieving a stable harmony between them. In sum, such relationship does not lead to anything close to a final equilibrium.

The Pulsating Paradox at the Heart of Subjectivity

In this unavoidable paradox, the virtual worlds carried by the extrapersonal-extrasensorial-extrapsychological experience of the forces clash with the current cartographies that are accessed by the personal-sensorial-psychological-cultural experience of reality in its actual forms. Such clash between those paradoxical experiences provokes a sensation of strange-familiar—a state that frequently emerges because the pulsating tension that causes it is inherent to life as a varying diagram of forces and their connections, which implies life's need to be materialized in new shapes. As such, this tension reappears constantly while life lasts; furthermore, it fulfills a primordial function in the endless process of configuration and reconfiguration of subjectivity and its environment.

The paradox of the relationship between strangeness and familiarity destabilizes subjectivity's equilibrium, as there is something pulsating in its experience that cannot be incorporated by its actual modes of existence and their codes, the images it has of itself, as well as of its world. A state of uneasiness takes hold of subjectivity and raises a question mark that it will need to respond to in order to recover equilibrium. Such malaise is a fundamental element of life in its human version: it works as an alarm that calls desire to act each time life's new diagram of forces produced by new encounters of bodies cannot breathe in its current forms and needs to be actualized in new ones. This process can be unleashed by encounters that potentiate life, as well as by those that decrease its strength. Desire is then driven to choose points in the topological-relational surface of the world to connect itself—points in which it will make its cuts in order to give back to subjectivity a contour, its consistency, and its meaning, allowing it to recover a balance, always provisional.

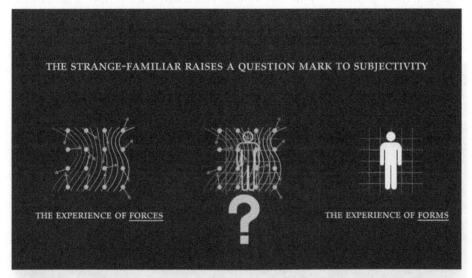

THE STRANGE-FAMILIAR RAISES A QUESTION MARK TO SUBJECTIVITY

THE EXPERIENCE OF FORCES

THE EXPERIENCE OF FORMS

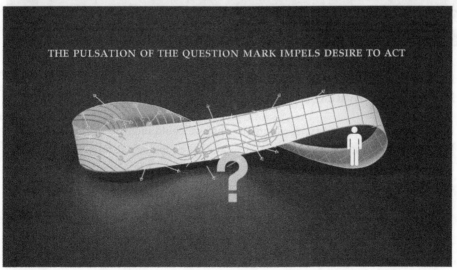

THE PULSATION OF THE QUESTION MARK IMPELS DESIRE TO ACT

The act of cutting is therefore the thinking practice of desire, which, motivated by the tension of the strange-familiar, produces the forms of reality and its representations. In other words, the cuts result in the unconscious formations in the social field, their existential territories, and their respective cartographies. Each of our actions is therefore an act of cutting of desire on the topological-relational surface of a world, a process that is interrupted only by death. It is precisely at the moment when desire is called into action that its diverging politics are told apart: they depend on the type of cutting that desire will opt for when facing the uneasiness that makes it move.

Now we can go back to the questions that were raised above regarding the end of the presentation of Lygia Clark's *Caminhando*: What happens in the experience proposed by this work? What gives it, or fails to give it, the status of an event? The idea is to expand those questions beyond this work, to problematize the politics of desire that do or do not lead to the creation of an event. This will be our instrument for analyzing the current state of things in the field of curatorial practices.

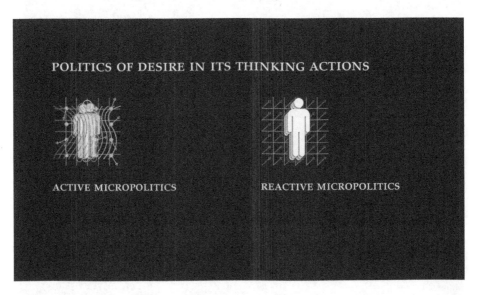

PERSPECTIVES OF DESIRE ACTIONS:
FROM ACTIVE TO REACTIVE MICROPOLITICS

Let us return to the two types of cutting that we could identify in the work of the Brazilian artist, but this time taking as support the topological-relational surface of the world. Considering that desire is what acts in human life, the intention here is to extract from this work indications of its potential power to deprogram the colonial-capitalistic unconscious or, on the contrary, to reproduce it to infinity.

Reactive Micropolitics and Its Moral Compass

As mentioned earlier, under the colonial-capitalistic regime of the unconscious the knowing-body is obstructed, and subjective experience is limited to the subject, its consciousness, its perceptions, and feelings. Reduced in this way, subjectivity cannot decipher the virtual world that has been generated in the body, which would need to be materialized through a process of creation. Thus, to find a new equilibrium, it simply reaccommodates the current cartographic codes and itself within them, so that everything goes back to the same place. Desire works reactively: to make its cuts in the surface of the world, it chooses points that had already been chosen. What gives orientation to this politics of desire is a moral compass. The forms that result from its actions are the outcome of an acritical identification of subjectivity with the dominant modes of existence. This is the outcome of a generic life, sterile life, deathlike life.

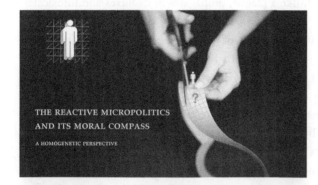

THE REACTIVE MICROPOLITICS
AND ITS MORAL COMPASS

A HOMOGENETIC PERSPECTIVE

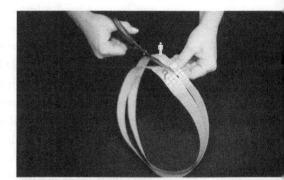

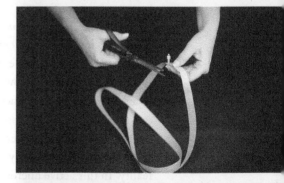

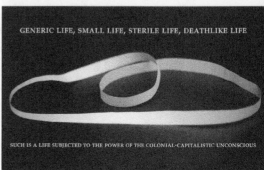

GENERIC LIFE, SMALL LIFE, STERILE LIFE, DEATHLIKE LIFE

SUCH IS A LIFE SUBJECTED TO THE POWER OF THE COLONIAL-CAPITALISTIC UNCONSCIOUS

In other words, the forms this kind of life produces are manifestations of its conservatism. This is the case even if they are full of creativity: when creativity is confounded with creation, its seductive power makes it more difficult to perceive that those forms are conservative, bearers of the colonial-capitalistic unconscious that lead to its reproduction. This becoming creative of desire's force of creation is one of the main operations of this regime of the unconscious, which turns life sterile.

In sum, the power of the colonial-capitalistic unconscious makes desire drift from its ethical course—a course that would result in concrete acts of creation, overcoming whatever interrupts the life process. In this way, desire is colonized, and the germinating potency of the life that moves it is drained to nourish the new field of "creative economy" and to extract from it economic, political, and cultural surplus value. The result of this draining of life is the stagnation of its continuous process of differentiation, producing a poison that, like a plague, propagates in its fluxes and intoxicates them.

This is the core micropolitical operation of modern Western culture, in its diverse unfoldings and developments—an operation that has been there since its origins and can be considered a historical pathology. In its current version, this operation has reached the utmost perversion and thrown us into the severe international crisis and and giving rise to the dangerous conservatism we are living with. In this extreme situation, we are trapped, impelled by the urge to shift out from this mode of subjectivation. This shift concerns not only its codes but also and above all the politics of its production, as the politics of production of desire and thought materialized in desire's actions. Without this micropolitical shift, everything returns to the established scenario. The urgency that this state of things imposes on us favors the sharpening of an awareness of the unavoidable need to embark on a work of micropolitical resistance, the effort to move ourselves from a reactive micropolitics toward an active one.

Micropolitical Resistance and Its Ethical Compass

Active micropolitics is oriented by an ethical compass that points desire toward the question mark posed by the uncanny and for which it must find an answer. Driven by this demand, desire acts toward the creation of something—a gesture, an idea, a text, or an artwork, but also a new form of existence, a new relation with the other, with sexuality, with work, and so on—in order to actualize the virtual worlds that inhabit the knowing-body. In other words, what is created by desire's actions in this case is a materialization of new ways of seeing and feeling, introducing new creatures within reality. In this active micropolitics, desire's actions multiply the forms of reality: they are acts of creation, generating becomings of the subjectivity, its existential territories, and their cartographies. The rebalancing, in this case, is found when the new diagram of life forces is embodied: as the new creatures carry with them the pulsation of those virtual worlds, they allow life to breathe again. This is the outcome of a noble life, prolific life, singular life, a life.

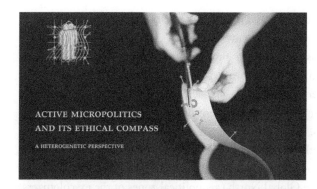

ACTIVE MICROPOLITICS
AND ITS ETHICAL COMPASS

A HETEROGENETIC PERSPECTIVE

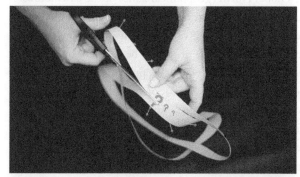

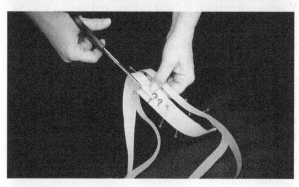

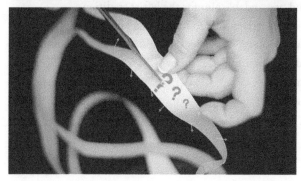

SUCH IS A LIFE THAT SEEKS
TO GET AWAY FROM THE
COLONIAL-CAPITALISTIC
UNCONSCIOUS

NOBLE LIFE, PROLIFIC LIFE,
SINGULAR LIFE, A LIFE

The needle of the ethical compass, which gives orientation to an active micropolitics, points to life itself. Thus, its focus is not a particular cartography with its moral codes but the essence of life as a continuous process of creation and differentiation, wherever it might be. It has no images, no words, and no gestures, because its aim is precisely to create them in order to embody life's movement.

The ethical compass is indispensable to orient desire if we really want to create post-colonial-capitalistic zones. Differently from a moral compass that guides some of the postcolonial theories, the ethical compass will not lead desire to choose the Global South (geopolitical zones of the ex-colonies and under the power of integrated world capitalism today) rather than the Global North (geopolitical zones of the ex-colonizers that have the power of integrated world capitalism today) as the point from which it will begin its cutting. The choice of desire in its active micropolitics does not work by opposing the geopolitical powers in the actual state of things: be it binary or dialectic, the opposition has as its reference the same logic of what it is opposing, the same politics of desire, the same regime of the unconscious. In contrast, oriented by the needle of an ethical compass, which points to life itself rather than acting by opposition, desire acts by creating a drift toward a different politics of production of individual and collective existence. Thus, the so-called decolonization depends on an active micropolitics, which leads us to an exit from the colonial-capitalistic unconscious, be it in the South or in the North, as they both belong to Western colonial-capitalistic culture and share the same unconscious regime. The idea of decolonization based exclusively on an epistemological shift, replacing the North by the South, is wishful thinking. Based exclusively on the subject's capacity of evaluation, which is reduced to the familiar (Western culture, in this case), and on the denial of the outside-of-the-subject capacity (the affect's power of evaluation), this position maintains the status quo, even if this might come from a leftist perspective. In fact, such reduction to a macropolitical perspective is the limit of the tradition of the political Left. The enormous world crisis we are living in today forces us to expand this tradition, introducing the micropolitical perspective. This is indispensable also to be more efficient in macropolitical struggles to increase social and economic justice, an essential and unavoidable aim for the leftist tradition.

The long detour we have made arrives here to its end. As said earlier, it was necessary in order to provide us with a magnifying lens to observe curatorial practices. But what does all this have to do with curating, and how will it allow us to pull apart distinct positions within this practice?

CREATING-CURATORS AND CREATIVE-CURATORS

The figure of the curator is directly related to all the above, because, as I mentioned at the beginning, it emerges in the context of financialized capitalism. Let us remember that in the internationalization of the new version of this regime, the mobilization of reactive micropolitics—a micropolitics that deviates desire from its creating destiny, its ethics—is refined and intensified. It is evident that this directly affects the field of art and is present in the new figure of the exhibition organizer, which, as mentioned earlier, adopts as one of its new functions mediating the negotiation between the interests of capital, of the institution, and of art. This makes curatorial practice a battlefield between different micropolitics, from the most active to the most reactive.

Now it is possible to describe the two fictitious curator figures, announced at the beginning as our main focus. As said, they would occupy the opposite extremes of the diverse range of perspectives involved in this field: the *creating-curator*, who occupies the active pole, and the *creative-curator*, the one at the reactive pole. Neither of these types exists in reality, as no position exists in a pure state; they are vectors of curatorial practices, which will be used as tools to problematize the current state of things in the field.

In an initial description, from a macropolitical perspective—that is, the one focused on the visible and the more obvious—what distinguishes these extremes is the position the curator assumes in the negotiation. In its reactive vector, the creative-curator tends to be the manager of the process of instrumentalization of art by capital. In its active vector, the creating-curator evaluates what is and is not negotiable, under the general criteria of maintaining the poetic force of the works and its contaminating potential.

The micropolitical position adopted in this force field is certainly present in the result of the curatorial project. But what is at stake in each of these curatorial micropolitics? What are the consequences of each of them in the reality where they intervene?

CURATORIAL MICROPOLITICS

What moves the creating-curators depends on constant work with themselves, which consists of resisting the power of the colonial-capitalistic unconscious over their own subjectivity. This is not achieved through theoretical or ideological training or through creating awareness of the macropolitical struggles or by mere goodwill. It consists of a subtle and complex work that implies making their own body vulnerable to the surrounding forces and listening to its effects in their outside-of-the-subject experience, as well as developing their own poetic ability to recreate themselves in their relation to the artworks and to the environment from this act of listening. Curatorial practice is what will allow them to render sensible the virtual worlds that inhabit them, which they access through their active knowing-body. For this they will have to create one or several dispositives that operate simultaneously or sequentially and that mobilize diverse elements, not necessarily or exclusively artistic.

How do they choose the artistic propositions they will bring together in their curatorial project, the new points where they will begin their curatorial cuts on the world's surface? Two possibilities are most common: either the virtual world inhabiting their own body is the starting point of their project, in which case they will look for works that resonate with it; or what will come first is their encounter with one or several works through which they connect with that virtual world in themselves, and this will impel them to conceive a curatorial project. Both movements can happen simultaneously, as even when starting from contact with one or several works it is not unusual to look for works by other artists that might resonate with them.

The creating-curators' challenge will be to invent dispositives of presentation and connection between the chosen works to create the conditions to make them operate in the present. In such a curatorial project, the seed of a world pulsating in those works will be able to germinate and gain an existential consistency in one or more exhibitions—and, eventually, in archives, texts, books, and other dispositives. When the curatorial action succeeds, the virtual world, which led it to be conceived is materialized, producing an event, becoming the current state of play. As such, the work of a creating-curator participates, in its own way, in the reinvention of the present.

It is important to state that the position of the curators, in its active pole, does not imply ignoring the importance of the institution and of financial investment in art. This would mean a regression to a marginal position for the artist and intellectual, to romantic, idealized figures that prevailed until the 1970s. On the contrary, in their active position, the curators fully assume their responsibility in this negotiation, first of all because, as said, creating-curators are always driven by a virtual world that needs to be actualized, generated by the effects of the forces that agitate the context from which the current state of art results; but also, and above all, because their action is not fully realized unless it is materialized in the territory where it operates. This means that they must negotiate with the art institution and the financial investment in art, accepting what is negotiable without giving up what is essential in art propositions, their poetic force, as mentioned.

ETHICAL COMPASS AND MORAL COMPASS IN CURATORIAL PRACTICE

The micropolitics at play in the actions of these two types of curator are distinguished by the compass that orients them. The actions of a creating-curator are oriented by an ethical compass, whose needle points toward life's demands as potency for invention of some worlds and dissolution of others, whenever this is necessary for its pulsation to continue. Marked by an active micropolitics, the creating-curator's actions participate in the reconfigurations of the cultural cartographies, as they are bearers of the poetic potency of art. What this type of curatorial practice tends to mobilize in its publics is the possibility of reconnecting with the knowing-body and listening to the affects and percepts—the same micropolitics that oriented its conception. In other words, the encounter with this type of curatorial practice potentially fosters in its publics a shift from the colonial-capitalistic unconscious.

In contrast, what gives orientation to creative-curators is a moral compass whose needle points toward the dominant cultural cartography. Their subjectivity is dissociated from its living condition and because of this, it can act only by reproducing the existing repertoire, in which they choose the points where they will make their cuts. They will opt for works that grant recognition: artists consecrated by the market and with media prestige, as well as those that investors and institutions are interested in promoting—in fact, all this tends to happen simultaneously. In the best hypothesis, the result of their practices will be a creative reshuffle of the dominant repertoire in the field of art, through which they will become celebrated characters within the creative economy scene.

It is worth pointing out that the creative-curators are those who, submitted to the colonial-capitalistic unconscious, introject the imaginary of social hierarchy. Conducted by this introjection, and normally belonging to the middle classes, they idealize the elites whose salons they cannot access, which causes them the feeling of humiliation. This leads them to fulfill the role of the mediator submitting to the interests of capital and the institutions that should be nonnegotiable in artistic practices—the disruptive power of their poetics, to which their subjectivity reduced to the subject does not even have access to, as it cannot deal with and thus must neutralize it. In this role, the creative-curators find an unexpected possibility of social climbing, all they cherish in order to free themselves from the anguishing humiliation that derives from their acritical identification with the place attributed to them within social and cultural hierarchy.

This opportunity came with the emergence of an elites' scene within integrated world capitalism, which involves having a collection of contemporary art, being part of the board members of the most prestigious European and North American museums, and doing tourism in international exhibitions and art fairs. This is one of the aspects that the elites of the most "provincial" countries idealize in their global peers, and they do as they can to imitate them. In Latin America this attempt tends to be pathetic. It is within this new international elites' scenario that emerges the caricaturesque figure of the glamorized curator as an unavoidable character. If the yuppie is the figure of subjectivity that gains force with the new regime and its creative economy, the creative-curator is its version in the field of art.

This figure tends to be impelled exclusively by its ego-narcissistic interests, its hunger for recognition, and, as said, for social climbing. As that tendency corresponds to the reactive micropolitics defining the colonial-capitalistic unconscious that drives our subjectivity, the creative-curators contribute to perpetuating it. What their practice will mobilize in the publics will be the same deafness to affects and percepts, the same obstruction of the knowing-body that has orientated them. And if, by mere chance, the artistic practices they choose to compose their curatorial project carry within them a poetic potential with a propagating force, it will probably be neutralized.

When the Curator's Unconscious Protests

If the colonial-capitalistic unconscious is at the base of modern Western culture, unblocking the affects and their power of evaluation is the unavoidable condition to effectively dislocate ourselves from this state of things. The artist who deserves such name has a privileged know-how for fulfilling this task. The curator needs to invent dispositives to keep active art's transformative potential, driven by an ethical compass that puts the curator's practice at the service of life. Showcasing the world from this perspective, the dispositives the curator conceives will be able to contaminate us, leading us to replace our moral compass with an ethical compass to guide our own actions. If the creative-curator vector is the yuppie of the arts, who has succumbed to the colonial-capitalistic unconscious and whose practices contribute to reinforcing this politics of unconscious in her/his publics, could we say that the creating-curator vector belongs to the unconscious that protests? If this makes sense, the creating-curator's practice would have the effect of expanding, within its publics, the field of the unconscious that protests.

As I wrote when introducing the description of these two curatorial figures, it is evident they do not exist as such in reality. As in every human activity, curatorial practice oscillates between several degrees of activity and reactivity. What matters is to be aware of this oscillation and to endeavor to break the fetish of the colonial-capitalistic unconscious, which continues to capture desire and deviate it from its ethical function, which consists of bringing the demands of life into existence.

In this sense, even though I am not familiar with the specific questions that are at stake for curators in the field of theater and performance, as I confessed at the beginning of this article, I welcome this seminar as a component of the "Show Me the World" multi-part project, as well as other projects and publications that have been conceived with the intention to think about curatorial practice in this area. Such initiatives signal that the figure of the curator is shaping up also in this field. If this is the case, the creation of conditions that allow those who act within this field to think collectively about the role of the curator will no doubt contribute to strengthening and disseminating the vectors of an active micropolitics in this new function. The field of theater and performance has the advantage of not having yet been so brutally instrumentalized by financialized capitalism as has the field of visual arts. Because of this, the preventive treatment such initiatives can perform is more than necessary. It might actually contribute to avoiding the contamination of this field by the epidemic of the creative-curators, who place their practice—and, with it, artistic practice—at the service of capital, reproducing and perpetuating its reactive micropolitics, against the political potency of art.

To conclude, I leave ten suggestions for those who, like me and many others, search for ways to decolonize the unconscious in their curatorial practices and beyond them. These suggestions should be reviewed, problematized, reworked, clarified, refined, expanded, deployed, multiplied, or simply suppressed.

Ten Suggestions for Those Who Search to Decolonize Their Curatorial Practice

1. De-anesthetizing the vulnerability to the forces and their variable diagrams: the potency of the subjectivity in its outside-of-the-subject experience

2. Reactivating the knowing-body: the experience of a world in its living condition (extrapersonal-extrasensorial-extrapsychological-extracognitive)

3. Unblocking the access to the tense experience of the strange-familiar

4. Not denying the fragility that results from the destabilization that the strange-familiar experience unavoidably promotes

5. Neither interpreting the fragility and its malaise as a "bad thing" nor projecting on it fantasmatic readings (premature ejaculations of the ego provoked by its fear of abandonment, rejection, repudiation, humiliation, and social exclusion)

6. Not giving in to the will of conserving forms and to the pressure it exerts against life's will to power (potency) in its impulse toward differentiation. Sustaining oneself on the tense line of this destabilized state until creating an utterance that is the bearer of the strange-familiar's pulse, actualizing the virtual world announced by this experience

7. Not running over the temporality of the process of creation to avoid the risk of interrupting the germination of a world, making this process vulnerable to being diverted to its expropriation

8. Not renouncing desire in its ethics of life affirmation, which implies keeping it fertile, flowing in its unlimited process of differentiation

9. Not negotiating the non-negotiable: everything that would obstruct life affirmation in its essence as force of creation. Learning to distinguish it from the negotiable: everything that could be accepted because it does not preclude the vital instituting force

10. Practicing thought in its full function: inextricably ethical, aesthetic, political, critical, and clinical. That is to say, reimagining the world in each gusture, each word, each relation, each mode of existence—whenever life requires it

Afterword

This text is dedicated to all the all the curators who, with their practices of creating (curatorial practices and beyond them), driven by the ethics of desire, try to revert, pervert, subvert, deprogram, deinstall, de-establish, undo, deconfigure, disable, disarm, bring down, deactivate, empty, defetishize, or simply quit the colonial-capitalistic unconscious.

Notes

1. Quote from "Le capitalisme mondial integer," a lecture delivered in 1980 by Félix Guattari during a seminar of the CINEL—Centre d'Initiative pour des Nouveaux Espaces de Liberté (Centre for the New Spaces of Liberty Initiative)—a collective founded in Paris during the autumn of 1977 who were against the repression of the Autonomy movement in Italy. CINEL participants decided to dissolve the collective in order to create the free radio *Tomate* in 1981, when the French state monopole of radio broadcast was annulated by François Mitterrand. The lecture was first published in Portuguese as "O Capitalismo Mundial Integrado e a Revolução Molecular" in a collection of Guattari's essays, *Pulsações políticas do desejo: Revolução Molecular*, ed. and trans. Suely Rolnik (São Paulo: Brasiliense, 1981). The quote has been free translated from Portuguese into English by Pablo Lafuente. (For the English translation of the conference Integrated World Capitalism and Molecular Revolution by Felix Guattari, see https://adamkingsmith.files.wordpress.com/2016/10/integrated-world-capitalism-and-molecular-revolution.pdf.)

2. Gilles Deleuze and Félix Guattari, "Sur Capitalisme et Schizophrénie," interview by Catherine Backes-Clement, published in L'Arc, no. 49, March 1972, 47–55. Included with the title "Entretien sur l'Anti-Oedipe," in Gilles Deleuze, *Pourparlers 1972–1990* (Paris: Minuit, 1990), 24-38; English ed.: "Gilles Deleuze and Félix Guattari on Anti-Oedipus," in Gilles Deleuze, *Negotiations 1972–1990* (New York: Columbia University Press, 1995), 13–24.

3. The financialization of capitalism started between the end of the nineteenth century and the beginning of twentieth, at the same moment—and not by chance—as the expansion of art exhibitions. The new capitalistic regime was consolidated after the First World War, and from mid-1970s on it acquired a worldwide power. Such power resulted from the acceleration of technological innovations and the advent of neoliberal states, which destroyed the welfare states that had been installed after the Second World War. It also allowed the total opening of local economies to transnational enterprises, which became the very international political power.

4. The notion of integrated world capitalism was suggested by Félix Guattari in 1980 at the CINEL's seminar mentioned in note 1 above. The author frequently mentions it in his subsequent writings.

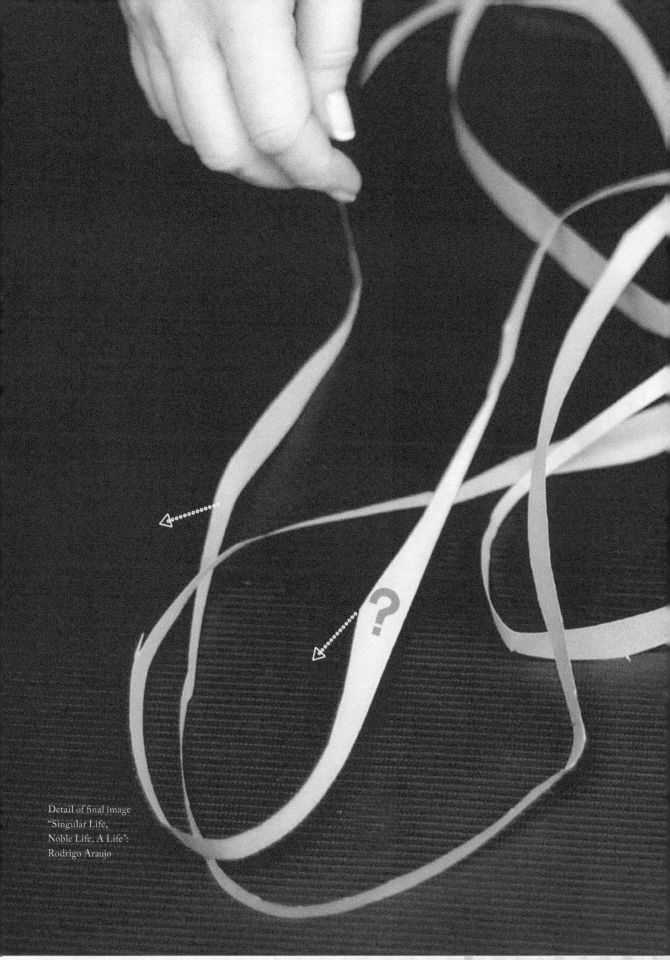

Detail of final image
"Singular Life,
Noble Life, A Life":
Rodrigo Araujo

Students from
the University of
Witwatersrand protest
tuition fee rises,
Johannesburg, 2015.
Photo:
Newzulu / Alamy

JAY PATHER

NEGOTIATING THE POSTCOLONIAL
BLACK BODY AS A SITE OF PARADOX

South Africa's recent wave of student protests was unprecedented in the postapartheid era both in scale and in the severity of the state's response. The protests arose in the midst of a series of global civic protests and have intensified in the past decade. The Fees Must Fall movement revolves around a number of endemic issues, from exorbitant tuition fees to a curriculum that remains, for the most part, trapped in the colonial paradigm.

The 2015 protests first gained prominence when University of Cape Town student Chumani Maxwele threw excrement at the statue of Cecil John Rhodes, situated at the time on the university's main campus. Maxwele, dressed in tights, enacted a carefully constructed performance that cut to the heart of an issue that remains unaddressed in South Africa today: the continued centrality of colonial symbology at South African institutions. For those who claimed that the statue was just part of a dormant history, the efficacy of the response that followed the image of the hallowed statue swathed in excrement challenged these assumptions and claims to long-gone memory and dormant oppression. The symbol of "people's shame" associated with the poor state of sanitation in South Africa's townships superimposed on one of the persisting bastions of colonial oppression occupying central space at the university seemed to expose the suppression of the pain of black people in the wake of the "rainbow nation" ushered in by Nelson Mandela.

Another profound symbol emerged at the height of the protests: the white human shield. Student protests at historically black universities, despite being largely under the radar, came into prominence at historically white universities. Initiated by a predominantly black group of students, the marches, demonstrations, and sit-ins quickly attracted white students. When police responded with brutality, white students were ushered to the front of the groups. This was meant to form a kind of buffer between

Theater 47:1   DOI 10.1215/01610775-3710477
© 2017 by Jay Pather

UCT student
Chumani Maxwele
addresses the crowd
at the removal of the
Cecil Rhodes statue,
Cape Town, 2015.
Photo:
Rofhiwa Maneta

UCT student Chumani Maxwele addresses the crowd at the removal of the Cecil Rhodes statue, Cape Town, 2015. Photo: Rofhiwa Maneta

the police and the black student body to stop police from using violence to disperse the large groups of students and quell the protest. This proved to be a successful strategy for the most part. The white human shield was both a poetic and tragic performance of the value of the black body.

Ironically, or perhaps inevitably, this intense period of protests and surrounding debate has been followed by a slew of racist incidents in South Africa. The combination of a poorly performing government, unchecked racist attitudes, and widespread access to social media has permitted this attack on the black body to grow. In one such incident, a woman named Penny Sparrow likened the presence of thousands of black people on Durban's beaches on New Year's Day to an invasion by monkeys. The backlash was passionate and severe. These events shed a stark light on the exemplar of reconciliation that South Africa was positioned to become for the world in 1994—a postcolonial, postapartheid nation, undergirded by the wholesale neoliberalization of Mandela's radicalism (as has often been done with Frantz Fanon's theorizing on race). The perpetuated image of the black body as "less than" against this backdrop of a "free" South Africa is the dialectic underpinning this article.

I began this essay before the Fees Must Fall protests erupted, and the intention of the original article was to illuminate the abnegation of black bodies and explore how it may be instructive in how we think about the curation of live performance—especially with black bodies. In light of the recent and ongoing demonstrations, the need for such a study is more urgent still. There are three overarching threads or continuums that I wish to consider in approaching the topic of the black body as a paradox: the curation of presence, blackness as absolute, and the notion of "gaze" and "the world" in the title of the project behind this symposium, "Show Me the World," for which this paper was originally commissioned.

THE CURATION OF PRESENCE

The curation of live art, of presence, is of course paradoxical—the immediacy and spontaneity of live art is inherently resistant to premeditated arrangement, such that its curation demands mechanisms that allow for an odd suspension of disbelief. From curating performances that are conventional, such as modernist dance, to those that are disruptive and anarchic, programming presence to meet the expectations of artists, audiences, management, and sponsors and the precise execution of presence for an audience at a specific time and place come hand-in-hand with compromise in the attempt to offer aliveness on demand, spontaneity on tap.

When one factors race and the human body, sometimes performing in foreign contexts, into this precarious mix, the specter of hermetically sealed, racially inscribed fairs that paraded black bodies as curiosities (fresh in our memories, having taken place just one generation ago in Brussels) may be hard to erase as a frame to the performing black body locked in a set of expectations. The curation of presence and the interplay between revealing and hiding the mechanisms behind the curating are an important overarching continuum.

BLACKNESS AS ABSOLUTE

Blackness of course is not absolute. Singular readings of the black body confirm a reductive colonial stereotype. Even the questionable Albert Memmi cautioned in *The Colonizer and the Colonized*: "The colonized is never characterized in an individual manner; he is entitled only to drown in an anonymous collectivity."[1] The delineated black body implies a special project, a particular brand that turns race into a category and a frame. And yet there is, at the same time, a naïveté in the representation of black experience—a skewed representation of blackness, or else the black body rendered entirely unseen, silent—that makes it necessary to think of blackness as a category, for the very purpose of showing up this invisibility, exclusion, and failure of nuanced representation. This tension between the desire to relinquish race as a classification and the need to retain it is an important one, made clear by Stuart Hall's reading of race as a "floating signifier" that can never be "finally fixed" but that is "subject to the constant process of redefinition and appropriation"—a multiple, contextual, complex variable.[2]

The Myth of the Postracial

For some, perhaps the most compelling direction in which race discourse has gone, and a crucial continuum in considering the black body and curatorship in the twenty-first century, is the capitulation to the idea of the postracial. Indeed, the concept of a society that exists beyond and apart from race is a wonderful fantasy, and in the quest to restore our fractured humanity it is a notion that warrants consideration. But given the prevalence of specific, directed assaults on the body of color, a state of being that is somehow "postrace" is no more than a fantasy.

Racial identity is a complex, iterative process, constantly in the making, subject to the vagaries of material and economic policies; it is not a fixed state of being to be transcended. Homi K. Bhabha touches on a similar idea, commenting on the dangers of a multiculturalist perspective that attempts to understand and thus contain cultural differences within a "particular universal concept."[3] This link between the idealism of the postracial and Bhabha's cautioning against a globalized utopia of universal sameness is crucial in helping us to separate our desires from the realities that artists present to us and vital in informing curatorial projects.

Show Me the ~~World~~ Gaze

What, then, is the "world" in the title of the project "Show Me the World"? Is it both a statement of generosity and arrogance—alluring and repugnant, expansive and reductive? Is it a statement of inclusivity, or does it imply another world out there to be absorbed into the dominant world? This act of othering, as we know, is one of the key difficulties we face in the curation of performance, especially of black experience and of works from the African continent.

Further, in thinking about our gazing of (or being gazed at within) this world, we need to remind ourselves that when we speak of race, we are of course talking about more than just the materiality of pigment; we are talking of power, economics, access, and agency. In whiteness studies, whiteness is not about skin; it may be a signifier or a notion that is performative, constituted as a largely invisible privileged cultural category. John T. Warren's *Doing Whiteness* brings us to understand the ways in which whiteness is reified and normalized.[4] In *Curating Inequality*, Andria Blackwood and David Purcell further argue that whiteness presents itself as a position of dominance, asserting that whiteness is maintained through the process of exclusion by establishing the white cultural narrative as both ordinary and invisible.[5]

Taking this notion of a dominant, racially inscribed cultural narrative that has been maintained and abetted over time, it becomes clear that these movements in and out of power structures by black people, and with it the performance of race and identity, started over four hundred years ago. Realities, languages, and cultural forms imposed on complex belief systems and traditions set up a denigration of self to varying and often violent degrees. For people of color, the presence of metanarratives appears long before the twentieth century; indeed, metaconsciousness was present at the onset of the colonial experience.

The implication of this, for curators, is a more pressing need to consider the expansiveness of the range of works by artists of color and to signal the differences and nuances that emerge from the key influential periods. The full range of precolonial, colonial, and postcolonial traditions and diasporas calls for far more complex kinds of showing and gazing than colonial spectatorship allowed—a showing where the world being gazed at was secondary to the construction and holder of the gaze. Most important, we need to consider psychic shifts in power and consciousness and the myriad ways in which the black body remade itself in relation to other, more powerful bodies. These cognitive shifts, brought about by intense upheaval, violence, and estrangement, inform much of the analysis that follows. The world of the black body, I argue, is inherently heterogeneous and more complex than has often been recognized. With these overarching continuums of curation of presence, blackness as no absolute, and the problem inherent in the statement "show me the world" as a basis, I turn now to explore the performing black body through the particular lens of a South African curator, offering an analysis that may extend to broader issues experienced in other parts of the world.

THE BLACK BODY: MEMORY, INERTIA, SPILLAGE

In a 2012 exhibition titled *Hail to the Thief II*, Brett Murray, a white South African artist, exhibited *The Spear* at the Goodman Gallery—a high-profile, contemporary art gallery in Johannesburg. In the painting, President Jacob Zuma's face is inserted on a poster resembling the classic Victor Ivanov poster *Lenin Lived, Lenin Is Alive, Lenin Will Live*. In Murray's work, however, Zuma's genitals are exposed. Zuma and South Africa's ruling party, the African National Congress (ANC), issued an application to the courts calling for the painting to be removed, due to the personal injury it had caused the president.

In the midst of the court case the painting was vandalized and destroyed by two men, Barend la Grange and Lowie Mabokela, and by coincidence, national broadcasting agency eTV happened to be interviewing the gallery manager about *The Spear* at the time of the incident. Camera operators turned to film the defacing instead, and the footage was broadcast nationwide that evening. The attack might be read as a neat, rehearsed performance—la Grange, a white man, placed two crosses over the face and genitals depicted in the painting, while Mabokela used black paint to expunge the rest of the figure. La Grange and Mabokela were unknown to each other, and in the subsequent handling of the two men, the footage reveals something further about the distinct treatment of white bodies and black bodies: la Grange was chided, politely taken aside, and handcuffed; Mabokela was man-handled, head butted, and thrown to the floor with his hands behind his back. Almost immediately thereafter, public response to the attack and to the artwork itself (expressing both condemnation and support) erupted, the height of which was the image of the president's lawyer, Gcina Malindi, weeping as he tried to articulate the links among race, poverty, apartheid, and censorship. A large group of ANC supporters marched to the Goodman Gallery. Subsequently composer and singer Simphiwe Dana wrote in a blog post addressed to the editor of *City Press*, Ferial Haffajee:

> Yes, Zuma is the worst president and he has set back the feminist movement, but we can't sacrifice one struggle for another. . . .
>
> People are angry at Brett Murray at daring to think that he, as a white man, a descendant of an oppressive regime of slave owners and land thieves, the cause of our dehumanization, has a right to depict us in a dehumanizing manner under the guise of free speech. I vaguely remember at the height of the Zimbabwe uprisings, there was an online game depicting Mugabe as a baboon being fed bananas. It was a personal affront to me; it blatantly played into evil colonial stereotypes. Such is the case here as well. The image of a black man with his penis hanging out on display in galleries, plastered all over the internet, in your newspaper for our children to see, for the whole world to see, shifted something in me. An animalistic howl died in my throat, perhaps a gene memory flashback coupled with the reality of my existence today. It felt like giving birth to death. Like this new SA is stillborn. This hurt is deep.[6]

And cultural theorist Achille Mbembe observed:

> The controversy surrounding the exhibition of President Jacob Zuma's private parts has not only unleashed a torrent of emotions and passions. It has also released high levels of negative and at times toxic energy.
>
> What has irked many is not the desecration of President Zuma's genitals as such. What has irked many is the fact that once again, the black body (of which Zuma's has become in the cipher in this instance) is the repository of all the anxieties, neuroses, phobias, and sense of estrangement of white South Africa. What has irked many is the realisation that, after twenty years of freedom, the black body is still a profane body. It still does not enjoy the immunity accorded to properly human bodies.[7]

The desecration of a painting exposing the penis of a black man, the president, by a white artist inside of a white-owned gallery is a performative gesture—a quintes-

The statue of
Cecil Rhodes is
removed, Cape Town,
2015. Photo:
Rofhiwa Maneta

sentially South African moment when the surface of reconciliation and the sheen of
normality are forced to give way to probing questions about art, ownership, the body,
culture, and race. These questions erupted with a violent intensity when ANC supporters marched to the Goodman, threatening to burn it down. A seemingly innocuous
middle-class gallery space dedicated to contemporary art became a symbol of oppression for the largely working class, a heady performance of the racialized body in several
manifestations.

This incident—a microcosm of the forms of subjugation inscribed on the black
body—needs to be viewed in a wider context. It must be viewed against the backdrop of
the Marikana massacre in South Africa, when thirty-four black miners were shot and
killed while protesting for a living wage twenty years into our democracy; in relation to
the contemporary killings of black men by white policemen across the United States of
America; and against the disproportionately high rates of incarceration of black men in
the United States. Each of these "moments" has reopened the association of blackness
with crisis. Dana's description of her response to *The Spear* as a gene memory flashback
and Mbembe's comment that the image of the black body as profane persists lead me to
an examination of memory.

Memory

Memory as discourse has pervaded much performance and critical theory for several decades. In South Africa as discourse that goes beyond nostalgia for those moments in the 1990s of reconciliation and the promise of equality among all peoples, it is much contested and vigorously alive in our consideration of blackness. The holders of South Africa's wealth and land remain largely unchanged since apartheid. There is an alarming disparity between the wealthiest and the poorest sectors of the population, and the number of people living on the poverty line has barely changed since apartheid. Greg Nicolson writing in the *Daily Maverick* surmises that "53.8% of people . . . fall under the widest definition of poverty in South Africa, surviving on under R779 ($47) per month."[8]

In South Africa, then, the act of recalling the violent past immediately and directly invokes the present, for the lack of substantial change in our material circumstances demands a perpetual resurrection of what went before. This interrogation is not merely a matter of confession and closure (in the manner of the Nuremberg and Rwanda trials); instead, it is a necessary journey to express frustrations and to account for the current economic distress, poverty, and wretchedness. As is often alluded to in the works of Jacques Lacan, Paul Ricoeur, and Michel Foucault, the act of remembering in South Africa is very much an obsession not with the past but with the present.

In their seminal article "Symbolic Closure through Memory, Reparation, and Revenge in Post-conflict Societies," psychologist Brandon Hamber and anthropologist Richard Wilson observe that this inextricability of past and present is precisely what South Africa's Truth and Reconciliation Commission sought to suppress, since the discourse of healing, reconciliation, and unity and the heralding of a new dispensation are premised on a break from the past:

> The nation-building discourse of truth commissions homogenize disparate individual memories to create an official version, and in so doing they repress other forms of psychological closure motivated by less ennobled (although no less real) emotions of anger and vengeance. Claims to heal the collective unconscious of the nation therefore mask how truth commissions both lift an authoritarian regime of denial and public silence, as well as create a new regime of forgetting which represses other memories and forms of psychological closure.[9]

Anthony Bogues is also concerned with the role of memory in the performance of the black body in dominant discourse, characterizing the black body as a disposable but required thing—a notion he derives from Aimé Césaire. In an address at the Southbank Centre in July 2015, Bogues spoke about recalling the black body as a source of fright and therefore one that is in need of tutelage, to be disciplined and subjected.[10] He contended that the brazen objectification and silencing of black bodies in the Marikana

Students stand on the pedestal that once held the statue of Cecil John Rhodes, Cape Town, 2015. Photo: Roger Sedres / Alamy

massacre were precisely about putting an end to fright.[11] The same might be said of the fatal shootings of black men by white American policemen.

Invoking Foucault's notions of the archaeology of knowledge, material traces left behind, and memory that grapples with this, Bogues asks us to turn our attention away from the object of our gaze to the archaeology of the gaze, to excavate what it is that frightens us, or what is it that we remember. Accepting that violence can create somatic trauma—where memory is nothing more than "fleeting images, the percussion of blows, sounds and movements of the body—disconnected, cacophonous"[12]—the demand to adopt a contrived civility in proper society, while harboring such a trauma-tized, disparate sense of self, is to wear what Fanon perceived as the divided self: "For it is implicit that to speak is to exist absolutely for the other. . . . The black man has two dimensions. One with his fellows, the other with the white man. A Negro behaves dif-ferently with another Negro."[13]

At the Gordon Institute for Performing and Creative Arts (GIPCA) 2014 Live Art Festival,[14] artist Chuma Sopotela presented *Inkukhu ibeke iqanda* (*The Chicken Has Laid Its Eggs*). Her work demonstrated an approach to the body that was formal and struc-tural as well as visceral. Set phases and clear spatial demarcations of the performing area created a taut vehicle for a largely improvised performance. At one point, Sopotela defaces the walls of the Cape Town City Hall with cow dung, writing "Nkandla" with the fermenting dung.[16] She later removes a South African flag from her vagina. Both acts may or may not be repeated in subsequent performances. Sopotela's performed rit-uals, realized through daily meditations, become a means of creating meaning through fragmented and fleeting reenactments. As a result of their repetition, memories are triggered that in turn become pathways followed through in improvisation and perfor-mance. The body becomes a repository of memory—re-presented, fragmented, incho-ate, and violent.

Themba Mbuli's *Dark Cell*, presented at the 2012 Live Art Festival, explores the black body as a site of inherited trauma.[17] Like Sopotela, Mbuli utilizes a formal frame with large-scale projections of images of political prisoners on Robben Island—the backdrop to a performance that descends into a hellish excavation of incongruence and fractured psyches. His anxious, dissociative state recalls Fanon's self-division and "two dimensions" of the oppressed body—at once agreeable and disobedient, pliable and vio-lently resistant.

Inertia

While memory and a traumatic past bleed inevitably into the present—a present that reenacts the deprivations of the past and allows memory its visceral, graphic reimag-ining—a grip on the future is much more tenuous. South Africans live in a slippery state of postponed gratification by the real fruits of a democracy so hard won. The future resembles a suspended malaise of broken political promises and a rapidly wan-ing patience with national projects of social cohesion. The good life that government repeatedly urges its citizens to look toward renders present-day reality a kind of unreal-ity—a distension, a floating above the ground. The constant rupturing of the narra-tive of material progress and development, articulated at the onset of our democracy in 1994, reinforces a state of stasis, impotence, and inertia. The profound economic asymmetries that persist in South Africa, characterize our lived reality with a kind of schizophrenia, where the overwhelming presence of despair and the very human need to cling to hope gnaw away at each other.

It is not surprising, then, that absurdity—where the black body is devoid of reason and purpose—pervades a great deal of performance art in South Africa. Even at the height of apartheid, much of the protest theater that emerged from South Africa (epitomized by the work of Mbongeni Ngema, Matsemela Manaka, Maishe Maponya, John Kani, Winston Ntshona, and Athol Fugard) evoked a black body that was dehumanized and yet that found a poetic reintegration and reconstruction of spirit in envisaging the end of struggle and in the romance of the good and noble fight. Increasingly, however, South African artists are evoking a black body without coherence or logic, reminiscent of the responses to fascism by European artists in the early twentieth century among the dadaists, futurists, and later the Theatre of the Absurd.

Choreographer Ntsikelelo "Boyzie" Cekwana's work, for instance, is frequently characterized by the non sequitur and the combination of slapstick comedy with violent imagery, philosophical text, and a stripped-bare contemporary dance language.[18] Cekwana's *In Case of Fire, Run for the Elevator*, performed at the GIPCA 2014 Live Art Festival, tells a story of "food and its intricate, uneven and invisible poetics."[19] Told through three characters representing love, power, and privilege, it is a story of food as a representation of difference—a shared need unequally met. Cekwana dissects authority while presenting what he describes as

a silent musical of rhythmic interventions to a score heard only by the interlocutors . . . a tawdry essay on the disquiet of an angry stomach grumbling at the deafening din of culinary correctness. *In Case of Fire* is an attempt to run for the elevator in the midst of an inferno concocted by the misadventures of a rather misguided crew attempting to escape the confines of serious art. The work honors imbecility and pokes fun at heroism, authority and the republic. It flirts with ambitions of legitimacy as it scours the uncertain terrain of artistic acceptability.[20]

In *Complicated Art for Dummies*, performer Ntando Cele appropriates a white alter ego, Bianca White, to explore issues of power and prejudice.[21] Bianca White claims to be from Rhodesia (present-day Zimbabwe) and is an experienced talk show host and world traveler with an extensive knowledge of the European art scene. In Cele's words, Bianca White implores: "Forget about TED talks, this is the voice of success with a sharp analysis of what is lacking in African art and the European need for suffering."[22] The portrayal comes replete with full makeup, a blonde wig, and an attempt at an English accent. There are moments when White seems to lose control and we witness Cele attempt to reassert herself, refusing to be obliterated. Absurdity and impotence alternate with a depiction of the grotesque as Cele uses facial contortions and her own features to play with ideas of mask, burlesque, and the schizophrenic black body.

Spillage

Chumani Maxwele's historic flinging of excrement on the statue of Cecil John Rhodes at the University of Cape Town brings to light a further aspect of the black body that warrants exploration: spillage and overflow. That the response to the extremities of a failed democracy and the failure to provide security for the black body have often been expressed as spillage, interruption, and overflow is, I propose, a consequence of an almost Kantian project of reason and restraint that has characterized a great deal of work on the body, memory, and heritage over the past twenty-two years.

The call to reason pervades Mandela's post-1994 legacy epitomized by projects such as the Truth and Reconciliation Commission, the original Government of National Unity, social cohesion, and the ideal of equality in diversity. These were good intentions, intended to heal those that suffered under and benefited from an unjust system, and focused on reconciliation and forgiveness rather than redress. The fallacy of achieving a harmonious state of existence without the commensurate redistribution of resources has been explored elsewhere in this article.

Responses to this constructed gentrified fantasy thrust upon a postapartheid nation have increasingly emerged from what we might call the realm of the sublime—the chaotic overflow and spill evident in the service delivery strikes that occur almost daily in South Africa. It manifests, too, in the consistent walkouts by the opposition party, the Economic Freedom Front (EFF), during parliamentary sessions. In the 2015 State of the Nation Address, security personnel physically assaulted EFF members in Parliament.

The launch of the Rhodes Must Fall movement with the throwing of excrement further illustrates an excessive spillage of shame, another searing example of spillage and overflow in a time of extremities. The writing of Sarah Lincoln is instructive here. She encompasses ideas around waste and overflow into her analysis of postcolonial African literature (Ayi Kwei Armah, Ben Okri, Ngui wa Thiong'o), reading these authors against Africa's "continued status as a 'remnant' of globalization—a waste product, trash heap of disposable raw material, and degraded offcut of the processes that have so greatly enriched, dignified and beautified their beneficiaries."[23] Lincoln contends that "the 'excremental' vision of African authors, artists, poets and filmmakers reflects their critical consciousness of the imbalances and injustices that characterize African societies and polities under pressure from monetized capitalism and domestic corruption. The figure of superfluity, excess, destruction or extravagance—concepts gathered together under the sign of 'waste'—is a central thematic, and indeed a formal feature of many postcolonial African works."[24]

In the excess of Maxwele's actions, there is the suggestion of material realities that, no matter the obfuscation, will ultimately emerge. The volatile energy of these extreme symbolic acts of disclosure, which seem to occur suddenly and sporadically, seems to be a search for a response that matches the weight and pressure and gravity of

Chuma Sopotela's
*Inkukhu ibeke iqanda
(The Chicken Has
Laid Its Eggs)*, Cape
Town City Hall,
Cape Town, 2014.
Photo: Val Adamson

the sustained silence—maybe even not a search at all but a natural, inevitable seeping through and overflow of emotion, given form in the body and its waste.

With the Rhodes statue itself, there is also the notion of it as a symptom of a disease, a symptom that you do not or should not really notice. It is, after all, something students and lecturers black and white have been passing without incident for twenty-two years of democracy. The attack on what many have inscribed as a harmless piece of concrete is about spillage. The attack on an abiding presence, as a symptom of a silence, of the unspoken pervasiveness of the colonial legacy at the university, reminds us of the disease that the liberal tradition in this country is no longer able to contain and explain in the languages of politeness and gentrification. These are, after all, the innocuous building blocks of liberal thought, wrapping up and hiding the persistent colonial project in cultural signs that appear harmless, inert, and incapable of harm by the fact that they are often just aesthetic objects.

Visibilities and Invisibility

At a 2015 event in Brussels (SIGNAL no. 5, Urban Interventions) I was struck by the reticence of speakers and audiences alike to use the word *black*, on the grounds that this was a potentially alienating and divisive term. On a number of occasions audiences used the word *immigrant* or *refugee* to replace *black*. It made me wonder if this forced absence of blackness was a part of the assimilationist tendencies of multiculturalism, an offshoot of a rampant universalist project that casts blackness as depersonalized and indistinctive. This might be seen as a good thing, except that it emerges from a space of dominance and control—agency and access are framed by white experience, and black people are welcomed or expected to simply fit in.

At a symposium at the University of Cape Town's Centre for African Studies in October 2015, a Norwegian academic referring to performance art works by black African artists dismissed the nudity that some artists employed as a strategy in their work around black skin as simply "a trend in Europe in the seventies." The implication was that the use of nudity by contemporary black artists was derivative. I find the statement very provocative. Does it suggest color blindness and the perception of the abject nude performing body (black or white) as a neutral body—simply a trend in the narrative development and evolution of art form? Or does it suggest a refusal to acknowledge the resurgence of the black body in crisis, where nudity is a particular strategy with a specific context?

Implicit in the consideration of race are the tensions between visibility and invisibility—the necessities of inclusion that a broad worldview entails, and at the same time the dangers of spotlighting blackness as a peculiarity that needs to be curated in a particular way. Hall's observation in "Why Fanon? Why Now? Why *Black Skin, White Masks*?" is instructive: "[There is an] almost irreconcilable tension in postcolonial studies between Fanon's spectacular demonstration of the power of the racial binary to *fix*, and Bhabha's equally important and theoretically productive argument that all binary systems of power are nevertheless at the same time, often if not always, troubled and subverted by ambivalence and disavowal."[25]

Brett Bailey's *Exhibit B* brings to the discussion the problematic hypervisible black body. *Exhibit B* is a performance installation by Bailey, a white South African artist, that sets black actors in a series of live scenes of enslavement reminiscent of the human zoos of the nineteenth and early twentieth century that audience members are permitted to view one by one. *Exhibit B* thus reenacts the abjection of the black body drawn from slave and anthropological exhibition discourses. As Bailey described it when the work toured Belgium: "I'm bringing five performers with me. The others are Africans living in Brussels. Some of them are asylum-seekers. And yes, I do put them in glass displays and cabinets and things like that. One by one, the spectators go in and do a tour."[26] In a BBC video, Bailey explained: "I am a performance maker. I come from South Africa. I am interested in beauty and the objectification of people, turning them into beautiful objects. I am very interested in the seductive quality of beauty, then also in what lies behind that beauty and the horror that is there."[27]

Does Bailey's work ask us to look at the contemporary black body as neutral—as any other body, all beautiful bodies, able to take on various guises? Is this representation closer to the "regular" body that the black body aspires to and not the profane one as Mbembe calls it? These questions may well posit *Exhibit B* as an instigator for productive debate, but there are several problems here, and I want to mention two. The first is the assertion that the black body is neutral, a part of the "objectification of people," while drawing attention to the physical qualities of blackness—skin, hair, passivity, and so on—that speak directly to the subject of slavery. It should be noted that the actors in *Exhibit B* never speak; they remain silent. The second contradiction of Bailey's installation is the conflation of horror with beauty. It is hard enough to scale past the objectifying gaze on the black body, but to then invoke Bailey's use of *beauty* (perhaps intended as equivalent to pathos, vulnerability, passivity?) as an anesthetizing agent for horror is abhorrent.

Knowing Bailey personally, I do think he has a penchant for overstatement—to go for the jugular, so to speak, by shooting down politically correct tropes. In the case of *Exhibit B*, however, there is a certain ossification and resultant numbness in the representation of the black body, and it is here that the piece is most harmfully problematic. The truly dehumanizing effect of *Exhibit B* is that the installation locks the black body in a stereotype of powerlessness and passivity and asserts that this state of imprisonment is unalterable. In the silencing of the actors, the notion of a complex life beyond the oppressed moment seeps away. Locked in the gaze of hypervisible abjection, the black body is not redefined but becomes merely inert matter for the gaze. The context of the gaze in contemporary galleries may indeed differ from the nineteenth-century spectacles—it is likely an agent for catharsis for white audiences (as was the case for the predominantly white audiences who attended the South African version I witnessed). But the black body nevertheless remains to be gazed at.

Bhabha's reflections on the 1994–95 Whitney Museum exhibition *Black Male* are instructive for thinking about how stereotypes function in *Exhibit B* as an enactment of the inevitable. Bhabha saw *Black Male* to be "afflicted by a kind of stasis: it gets mired in the visual logic of stereotypical identification. . . . I felt that despite the irony and the inversions, something of the rigor mortis of the stereotype had seeped into the show itself . . . there is life outside and beyond the stereotype, even for its victims."[28] This tension seems key to understanding the outrage provoked by *Exhibit B*—the exhibited specimen in her hypervisibility is simultaneously invisible by virtue of her indistinguishableness from the collection of oppressed black bodies that surround her.[29]

In a different but applicable context, Okwui Enwezor remarked in "Reframing the Black Subject": "More than alerting us to how the stereotype fixes its objects of desire in that freeze-frame of realism, as prior knowledge, the work of these artists exacerbates the stereotype by replaying it, perhaps unconsciously, as if it had always been factual."[30] Bailey's use of blackness made hypervisible—where the allure and repulsion of blackness aestheticized for consumption by a predominantly white audience are fixed in an unwavering gaze—is both simplistic and opportunistic. The simplicity lies in the choice of a path of least resistance for the audience, sealed in a modernist hermetically sealed construct. Using this simplicity to prompt feelings of guilt and temporary catharsis—where the act of paid viewing may be confessional in nature—is opportunistic.

It may be useful to juxtapose Bailey's installation with the work of an artist preoccupied with issues of hypervisibility, the gaze, and the black body. Tebogo Munyai is a performance artist who lives in Khayelitsha, a semiformal township on the outskirts of Cape Town. In his work *Qina ke Qawe* (performed at the 2012 GIPCA Live Art Festival, University of Cape Town), Munyai paints himself a shiny, deep black and begins the performance with a lit candle in his anus and a series of movements that replicate stereotypical positions of abjection. As the work progress, these movements are countered with moving dances of vulnerability and rage, followed by a section of serenity and calm.

Another of Munyai's works, *Right Inside* (performed at GIPCA's LAND Symposium, Grand Parad, Cape Town), comprises the relocation of several shacks from the shack settlement to the middle of the city, where they are then reconstructed. Inside these closed, tiny, four-walled shacks several performers enact a range of different scenarios through ritual, voice, and dance. Intimately concerned with the invisible/hypervisibility paradox, however, Munyai does not present such an easily consumable performance. Instead, the audience is locked out of what is going on inside the shacks and only able to catch glimpses of the performances through a few tiny holes drilled into the corrugated iron walls. Roused by the occasional scream or song or simply by silence, audiences must peer through the holes to access the performance, knowing perhaps that they are likely looking through bullet holes. It is a telling, ironic, self-consciously induced voyeurism. It is also emotive and affecting because when the audience feels that they have had enough or cannot bear the awkwardness of the viewing, they walk away.

In this work, viewers are also simultaneously conscious of watching other audience members watching the scene and of being watched themselves. While the construction and framing of the event is deliberate and clear, and the artist's hand is present, allowing a kind of distance from the events inside the reconstructed shacks, the weight of responsibility to stay or leave rests heavily on the viewer. Munyai's relocation

Themba Mbuli's *Dark Cell*, Cape Town City Hall, Cape Town, 2014. Photo: Val Adamson

and perversion of these "slices of life" (already relocated and dislocated historically) rendered hypervisible in *Right Inside* ask us to look again in a way that Bailey fails to do. Munyai affords contemporary agency and ensures that the subjects of his work move, emit sound, relate with one another within varying power dynamics, and inhabit an environment with complexity. As an audience member, I was the stereotype—singular, partial, and disconnected. If I wanted to change that, I would need to do much more than simply consume a performance. It would seem that, in the making visible of the black body, how the gaze operates and how (and why) agency is conceived in relation to the black body become paramount.

CURATING CRISIS

In approaching the black body as a paradox—both triumphant and vulnerable—artists have often presented blackness as a site of crisis. In thinking about the black body in crisis, it may be useful to think in terms of a constant ebb and flow of recovery and catastrophe: recovery seldom holds fast, and the specter of a postcolonial nation struggling to shake off the sophistication and pervasiveness of the colonial project serves as a persistent undercurrent. This unpredictability and volatility call for a reframing,

Tebogo Munyai's
Doors of Gold, Cape
Town City Hall,
Cape Town, 2014.
Photo: Val Adamson

wherein the regular assumptions of viewing are interrogated against the backdrop of constantly shifting sets of circumstances in the path to complete recovery of the human.

Some artists have taken these points of crisis and turbulence to extremes, which have challenged the norms of performance viewing. The challenge, then, is to curate such subversion, and so "curating crisis" becomes an act of contradiction in itself. Nonetheless, it may be useful as a starting point to suggest that the more self-conscious a process this curation is, the better. In other words, the revealing or exposing of the act of framing becomes imperative. The corollary is also true: to attempt to make such framing invisible and seamless signals, rather simplistically, that all is well in the world inside and outside the artwork of crisis. It is to conceal difficulties that the art world would prefer not to confront, but that we must.

The Tokolos Stencil Collective is a group of artists/activists based in Cape Town.[31] Although the individual artists in the collective have remained anonymous, their work has appeared, quietly and insidiously, in numerous public spaces. Most striking has been the repeated perversion of the City of Cape Town's slogan, "This city works for you," reinscribed in their work in several spaces throughout the city as "This city works for a few." In an unlikely acceptance of an invitation by an established gallery, the collective agreed to exhibit works at the Brundyn+ gallery in downtown Cape Town. The exhibition, titled *Plakkers*, was said in the gallery's press release to [bring] into conversation some of the many voices of visual dissent taking place in the city. "The wall" is a common motif in these artists' works, either as the site where the work is placed or as the very content of the work itself. As a versatile Afrikaans word meaning either stickers, decorators, squatters or pesters, *Plakkers* echoes this motif but also places the show within the vernacular register of everyday Cape Town news headlines where "land is invaded" and "squatters evicted."[32]

Tokolos Stencil installed an uncleaned portable toilet—a sight well known to black residents in Cape Town due to the city's failure to provide proper sanitation in informal settlements. In front of the installation was a single line reading: "There are none as invisible as those who wish merely to be seen." In the collective's own words: "Before leaving, we removed the toilet's lid and exposed art aficionados to the smell of decades of indignity and oppression meted out against Cape Town's poor."[33] The Brundyn+ management quickly shut the exhibition down and had the offending toilet removed. In response, Tokolos Stencil spray-painted the gallery's front walls with descriptors such as "Bourgeois Gallery" and "Dehumanisation Zone."

In her article "'Black Is' and 'Black Ain't,'" Nadine Ehlers reimagines crisis as a site of reformation of identity—a positive means to imagine and enact the racialized body.[34] The point of crisis is revisioned as a point of danger that proffers choices and could thus serve as a turning point. Artists such as Jelili Atiku, Bernard Akoi-Jackson, and Olaniyi Rasheed Akindiya have all used the black body in crisis in the manner Ehlers envisages—as an agent for disruption and interruption, sometimes violent, as well as a space for change. The possibility of representing crisis as a means of change is carefully navigated in these artists' works, and a fine tension is drawn between control and overflow, the predetermined and the shaped, rampant and spontaneous.

How does curation navigate authorship, artistic control, and overt and covert censorships in the meeting of audience expectation and the curation of a body in crisis? Ultimately, if curating is about "taking care of," our questions will have to address what it is that we care for—the audience, the artwork, the artist, the context, the concept, or the immersive experience? These questions and their relative weighting will inform the possibility of resolving the contradictions inherent in the attempt to curate crisis.

AUDIENCES, ACCESS, AGENCY

The concept of site specificity is generally associated with public art, the creation of public spheres, and audience participation in public spaces such as squares, waterfronts, and parks or spaces with open access such as pavements, railways stations, abandoned buildings, and shopping malls. But all art occurs in a specific site where the frame (the building, physical space, context, etc.) and the artwork interact with each other. These sites have a particular purchase, access, ownership, and codes of behavior that often predetermine its audience.

In the curation of static objects, there is every possibility of diverse publics being brought together to engage with the object. There is time and space for briefings and contexts. So an unfamiliar public may well be able to acquaint themselves with the codes and blend in. For ephemeral artworks that are scheduled at specific times, the issue of who knows when and where to be becomes a highly political one that entails access to information and historical realities of familiarity and belonging. This is important to consider if we wish to develop a conversation with audiences around race that is not unilateral, and if we wish to cultivate something much more complex and meaningful than a homogeneous audience familiar with the codes of the event.

If we accept that the world of performance lives somewhere between artist and audience, then a multiplicity of voices on both sides of the equation brings us closer to what this world may, should, or could be. To get around the eroticization of the other, the one-way consumption of poverty or crisis pornography, the public should ideally be plural—a panoply of publics that negotiate this gaze in rich and varied ways. The act of confronting race in terms of audience makeup already sets up a discourse around how a work is received. Instead of being informed by the intention of making for the other, a racially diverse audience invites the possibility for a textured and rich conversation with and among all kinds of publics and subjectivities. The intersection of publics is a crucial part in the creation and curation of a context around the black body.

Perhaps in "showing me the world" it is the world between the works that is most in need of revealing and investigating—texts and contexts that feed and enable works to be part of a milieu broader than the proscenium arch. Ultimately, then, it is the call for discursive, intertextual, intersectional experiences of performance and discourse that requires our response.

Conclusion

The resurgence of vulnerabilities in relation to the black body across the world marks difficult terrain. The quest for normalcy, for race to be invisible as a defining feature, is no doubt present in notions such as the postracial. But the languages of race continue to dominate because actions that are racially inscribed do. Achille Mbembe and Sarah Nuttall remind us in their article "Writing the World from an African Metropolis" that "the conceptual categories with which to account for social velocity on this continent, the power of the unforeseen and of the unfolding, are in need of refinement. So too is the language with which to describe people's relentless determination to negotiate conditions of turbulence and to introduce order and predictability into their lives."[35]

In South Africa, race resurges as an instigator of turbulence twenty-two years after democracy. The black body continues to navigate this turbulence as a receiver of this vast social velocity, not as yet located in circumstances that predictably and in an orderly way ensure the retention of its humanity. As Mbembe further observes, artists continue to probe urgently the question of languages and forms that give expression to such extremities. Curators face questions that are much more complex than aesthetic choice or intellectual context. Pressing and immediate events call for vigilance and doubt.

Despite our quest, in pursuing our work, for certainties, curatorial order, and the meeting of expectations, neat solutions and tied up endings seem to prove vacuous. In these moments—when such polarities as the demand for visibility and the ache to be invisible and slip away into the seductive arms of universal, postracial humanity; when present and past connect, collapsing time for the artist—it seems appropriate to be irresolute and suspended, to hold as an image, strong and uncompromising, the idea that this non sequitur, this lack of cohesion is what we have, all we have.

The distension expressed in the works I have referred to in this article is ultimately their enduring, if painful, life force and energy field. In these stuttering evocations, there is none of the body's release promised by democracy—let alone an entire civil rights movement. There is merely affirmation of a shifting present filled with inertia and a future that continues to elude. Apartheid and colonialism resurge not as obsessions with the past but as the persistence of vulnerabilities and crisis that surround the black body and remain as visceral as ever.

What are the mechanisms inherent in curation that could possibly render these contestations, spaces, and silences discursive and enabling? These gaps are present not just in land, home, place, are not just inscribed on skin, bone, organs, human tissue, but resonate time and time again in interrupted, incomplete memory. Coupled with persistent economic deprivation, migration, displacement, and the imposition of new world powers on a vulnerable continent, these inscriptions are never dormant or buried. They lie close to the surface of all our white and black skins, and for us as curators they demand forensic and unwavering attention.

NOTES

I want to express my gratitude to Catherine Boulle for her editorial contributions.

1. Albert Memmi, *The Colonizer and the Colonized*, trans. Howard Greenfield (Abingdon, UK: Earthscan, 2003), 000.

2. Stuart Hall, "Race, the Floating Signifier," Media Education Foundation, 1997, www.mediaed.org/assets/products/407/transcript_407.pdf (accessed October 4, 2015).3. Jonathan Rutherford, "The Third Space: Interview with Homi Bhabha," in *Identity: Community, Culture, Difference*, ed. Jonathan Rutherford (London: Lawrence and Wishart, 1990), 209.

4. John T. Warren, "Doing Whiteness: On the Performative Dimensions of Race in the Classroom," *Communication Education* 50, no. 2 (2001): 91–108.

5. Andria Blackwood and David Purcell, "Curating Inequality: The Link between

Cultural Reproduction and Race in the Visual Arts," *Sociological Inquiry* 84 (2014): 238–63.

6. Simphiwe Dana, "Sarah Baartmanisation Post Colonialism—South Africa," *Simphiwe Dana* (blog), June 10, 2012, simphiwedana.wordpress.com/2012/06/10/sarah -baartmanisation-post-colonialism-south-africa/.

7. Achille Mbembe, "The Spear that Divided the Nation," Brett Murray, 2012, www .brettmurray.co.za/the-spear-opinions/26-may-2012-amanda-magazine-professor -mbembe-the-spear-that-divide-a-nation/ (accessed September 2, 2015).

8. Greg Nicolson, "South Africa: Where 12 Million Live in Extreme Poverty," *Daily Maverick*, February 3, 2015, www.dailymaverick.co.za/article/2015-02-03-south-africa -where-12-million-live-in-extreme-poverty/#.VrinwLl94nV.

9. Brandon Hamber and Richard Wilson, "Symbolic Closure through Memory, Reparation, and Revenge in Post-conflict Societies," *Journal of Human Rights* 1, no. 1 (2002): 36.

10. Interestingly, the black body as a site of potential harm is derived from a tacit, covert acknowledgment that such a body has been subjected to so much debasement and extremity that it will—and indeed can only—respond in attack.

11. Anthony Bogues, "Thinking about Decolonization: The Archive and the African Body" (paper presented at the Sequins, Self, and Struggle Symposium, Southbank Centre, London, July 17–19, 2015).

12. Quoted in Anthony Bogues, "South Africa: On Becoming an Ordinary Country," *boundary 2* 34, no. 2 (2007): 185.

13. Frantz Fanon, *Black Skin, White Masks* (London: Pluto Press, 1986), 8.

14. GIPCA is an interdisciplinary institute in the University of Cape Town's humanities faculty. GIPCA's biennial Live Art Festival, started in 2012, is a festival dedicated entirely to performance art. It showcases innovative works by established and emerging local and international artists.

15. Chuma Sopotela, *Inkukhu ibeke iqanda* (GIPCA Live Art Festival, Cape Town, August–September 2014).

16. Nkandla is the private home of President Zuma, which became the source of immense public controversy in 2009 when it was uncovered that public funds, totaling R246 million, were used to make improvements to the compound. Nkandla has since become a symbol of government corruption and greed.

17. GIPCA, *Live Art Festival 2012 Programme* (Cape Town: Cape Town City Hall and University of Cape Town Hiddingh Campus, 2012).

18. Boyzie Cekwana, *In Case of Fire, Run for the Elevator* (GIPCA Live Art Festival, Cape Town, August–September 2014).

19. GIPCA, *Live Art Festival 2014 Programme* (Cape Town: Cape Town City Hall and University of Cape Town Hiddingh Campus, 2014), 26.

20. Ibid.

21. Ntando Cele, *Complicated Art for Dummies* (GIPCA Live Art Festival, Cape Town, August–September 2014).

22. Ibid.

23. Sarah L. Lincoln, "Expensive Shit: Aesthetic Economies of Waste in Postcolonial Africa" (PhD diss., Duke University, 2008), 4.

24. Ibid., 4.

25. Stuart Hall, "The After-life of Frantz Fanon: Why Fanon? Why Now? Why *Black Skin, White Masks?*," in *The Fact of Blackness: Frantz Fanon and Visual Representation*, ed. Alan Read (London: Institute of Contemporary Arts, 1996), 27.

26. Quoted in Michaël Bellon, "KFDA012: Brett Bailey Takes to the Courtroom," *BRUZZ*, May 3, 2012, www.agendamagazine.be/en/blog/kfda012-brett-bailey-takes -courtroom.

27. "Exhibit B: Introduction" [video] BBC, www.bbc.co.uk/programmes/articles/12ynx PVNKF1pYVrzZB9R2sM/exhibit-b-edinburghs-controversial-art-show (accessed September 1, 2015), at 0:25.

28. Homi K. Bhabha, "'Black Male': The Whitney Museum of American Art," *Artforum International* 33, no. 6 (1995): 110.

29. Bailey's installation sparked controversy around the world but elicited particular invective when it toured the United Kingdom in 2014. Protesters successfully campaigned to have the exhibition shut down at the Barbican in London, where it was scheduled to be shown in September 2014.

30. Okwui Enwezor, "Reframing the Black Subject: Ideology and Fantasy in Contemporary South African Representation," *Third Text* 11, no. 40 (1997): 37.

31. *Tokoloshe* in Zulu translates as "a mischievous and lascivious water sprite that causes trouble."

32. "Plakkers," Brundyn Gallery, www.brundyn.com/exhibitions/2014/plakkers/press/ (accessed September 1, 2015).

33. Tokolos Stencil Collective, "Real Art Makes the Privileged Uncomfortable," *GroundUp*, November 13, 2014, www.groundup.org.za/article/real-art-makes-privileged -uncomfortable_2444/.

34. Nadine Ehlers, "'Black Is' and 'Black Ain't': Performative Revisions of Racial 'Crisis,'" *Culture, Theory, and Critique* 47, no. 2 (2006): 149–63.

35. Achille Mbembe and Sarah Nuttall, "Writing the World from an African Metropolis," *Public Culture* 16, no. 3 (2004): 349.

Books

Michael J. Kramer

Dancing across the Proscenium

Dramaturgy in Motion: At Work on Dance and Movement Performance
by Katherine Profeta
Madison: University of Wisconsin Press, 2015

Katherine Profeta's *Dramaturgy in Motion* is really two books in one. It is an in-depth, almost ethnographic exploration of choreographer Ralph Lemon's work since the late 1990s, when Profeta joined him as dramaturg and he began a series of ambitiously multifaceted, research-driven, intercultural projects; at the same time, Profeta steps back to reflect upon dance dramaturgy more generally as a practice. Her book thus both exemplifies the dramaturgical—one could read it as a kind of extended magnum opus of a program note—and simultaneously seeks to explain more abstractly what the dramaturgical is in relation to choreographic creativity.

Profeta's study is at its most riveting when it successfully integrates the two foci, bringing the specifics of Lemon's own art into conversation with theoretical observations about what it means to pursue movement-based dramaturgy. In those moments, one glimpses how the dramaturgical has been crucial to what another dance dramaturg, Jenn Joy, describes as shifts in "the choreographic." Joy points to the transformation in recent decades from the writing of dance *on* bodies by choreographers to a far more adventurous experiment in designing movement *with* bodies through devised processes and collaborative creation. This she regards as fostering "the possibility of sensual address—a dialogic opening in which art not only is looked at but also looks back, igniting a tremulous hesitation in the ways that we experience and respond."[1] Within this context, it makes sense that dramaturgy, the theory and practice of dramatic composition, would become a part of choreography as it moves from being an act of imposition to one of discovery. The whole question of how to compose (or resist composing, or be met with resistance to composition by) bodies moving through space emerges. Indeed, various artistic, ethical, and political fault lines crack wide open as the previously ordered and constrained landscape of ballet, modern dance, and other dominant genres gives way. Choreography becomes suffused with myriad theoretical and practical concerns that, for many, only dramaturgy seems capable of addressing.

Over five chapters that focus on language and text, research, audience, movement, and interculturalism, Profeta takes up the matter of how dramaturgy might do so. Drawing upon memories, e-mail correspondence, notebooks, and other materials from her time with Lemon and his collaborators, she offers keen insights into what constitutes effective dance dramaturgy, as well as what continues to puzzle her. Her book joins a recent spate of essays and books about the topic, but it is the first full-length study of dance dramaturgy in particular.[2] That Profeta is among the first to address dance dramaturgy at length may come as a surprise since in the theater world as a whole the dramaturg is a long familiar, if controversial, figure. This is far less the case, however, with dance. Fortunately, Profeta is well positioned for the task of seeing dramaturgy as both old and new, long practiced and freshly invigorated. She was a founding member of the Elevator Repair Service theater company before joining Lemon and her own career has often crisscrossed between theater and dance, as well as between hands-on creativity and scholarly analysis.

Ralph Lemon's *The Geography Trilogy, Part 3: Come Home Charley Patton*, Walker Art Center, Minneapolis, 2005. Photo: Dan Merlo

As Profeta points out, the dramaturg was traditionally (and in many cases still is) the keeper of the history that shaped productions, or the in-house critic, or an institutional force shaping presentations, or some combination thereof. Since the 1960s, however, theatrical dramaturgy has become far more distributed across the members of a company and their collaborators. The move from the centralized role of one dramaturg to the decentered activity of "the dramaturgical" among many participants in fact parallels shifts in more avant-garde forms of choreography since the 1960s. Yet, as Profeta notes, the full migration of dramaturgy into the dance world is of fairly recent vintage. It was not until 1979, when Raimund Hoghe became dramaturg for Pina Bausch and her Tanztheater, that someone explicitly identified in the role (although as Profeta mentions in her book, long before Hoghe, dance dramaturgs existed without the name: the

Ballets Russes had its Sergei Diaghilev, George Balanchine had his Lincoln Kirstein, Merce Cunningham his long-running partnership with John Cage).

Only with Bausch did a particular person take on the job of dramaturg, yet this occurred at the very same moment that Bausch purposely destabilized the dominant place of both choreographer or dramaturg by asking her dancers themselves to enter more fully into dramaturgical-oriented choreographic tasks. There is an irony here: the dance dramaturg emerges as a discrete role precisely as the dramaturgical disperses itself across all the makers of a dance work. Perhaps this has to do with contemporary dance's funny urge toward mobility, something Profeta is intent to highlight in her book: the new figure of the dramaturg appears on stage, or, better put, backstage; the fruits of her labor quickly circulate to the rest of the ensemble. Since Bausch's groundbreaking work in the 1980s, dance makers have only grown more interested in areas of exploration that suit the dramaturgical. These include research-driven inquiry; cross-disciplinary endeavors that link dance to the visual arts, performance art, science, political activism, film, digital culture, and other fields; philosophical and conceptual issues; deconstructionist ideas; documentary-oriented approaches; and site-specific productions.

Dramaturgy in Motion, however, is not a critical history of dance dramaturgy. That book remains to be written, and it might adopt a more fully archival approach to historicize choreography's turn to dramaturgy in the context of late-twentieth-century art making, economic changes, and political shifts. While she includes a quick and effective historical overview, Profeta is far more interested in harvesting her interactions with Lemon to pursue a multidimensional and affirmational definition of the activities that define dance dramaturgy now. To be sure, she wants to describe what a dance dramaturg does with precision, but even then the terms proliferate. As Profeta wryly writes, when confronted by "a favorite relative, a curious student, a cocktail-party acquaintance," she maintains "a list of terms in mind that I can either support or refute, sometimes both in turn, as more specific models or metaphors for the dramaturgical role . . . researcher, editor, questioner, catalyst, historian, archivist, literary manager, outside eye, inside eye, advocate for the audience, advocate for anything *but* the audience, witness, midwife, gadfly, friend, and even amateur shrink" (14). In more academic circles, she also refers to the historical antecedents of theater dramaturgs such as Gotthold Ephraim Lessing and Bertolt Brecht.

Profeta refuses simplistic, reductive explanations of dance dramaturgy. "If it can be defined at all," she writes of the role of the dramaturg, it "can only be as a quality of motion, which oscillates, claiming an indeterminate zone between theory and practice, inside and outside, word and movement, question and answer" (xvi–xvii). Building on the work of prior practitioner-theorists such as Marianne Van Kerkhoven, André Lepecki, Heidi Gilpin, Myriam Van Imschoot, Hildegard De Vuyst, and Bojana Cvejić, Profeta seeks to "imagine the dramaturg as a figure engaged in a dance of entrance and exit, of play across the doorsill" that divides the rehearsal studio and the performance space from the larger world (16). For Profeta, the dramaturg, imported from theatrical traditions, becomes a kind of metaphorical (and sometimes literal) dancer herself. She moves. As a dramaturg *of* motion, Profeta most of all values dramaturgy *in* motion, hence her book title.

Lemon's work is fertile ground for Profeta's meditation on dance dramaturgy because he himself has often been a choreographer in motion. After the radical choice to disband his company in 1995, Lemon turned to intensive research and collaboration as the key modes to develop a series of interrelated projects. Profeta entered the picture in 1997 while still a student dramaturg at the Yale School of Drama. At that time, Lemon began work on the Geography Trilogy, which comprises *Geography* (1997), *Tree* (2000), and *Come Home Charley Patton* (2004). These were followed by *How Can You Stay in the House All Day and Not Go Anywhere?* (2010). In these works, Lemon asked intercultural questions of identity formation, traveling to West Africa and Asia before turning to the African American history in which his own family's story is implicated. He collaborated extensively and productively with dancers and musicians from non-

Ralph Lemon's *Geography*, Yale Repertory Theatre, New Haven, 1997. Photo: T. Charles Erickson

Western as well as nonprofessional backgrounds. He also sought out more unusual performance locations (the living rooms of the last living relatives of deceased blues musicians; museum galleries; and, especially perfect for a dramaturg, lecture-demonstration spaces). Additionally, he widened his forms of expression to include essays, talks, books, art installations, and films.

Probing Lemon's work from inside the process of its development, Profeta offers numerous insights. Since the dramaturg, with notebook in hand, often becomes the

representative of language in the dance world, Profeta hones in first on the continued fear that language and narrative reduce the power of physical expression. She believes that "the fear of the reductive, labeling power of language has not caught up to the last century of fiction writing, which has embraced the limits of linguistic meaning into its field of play, with techniques including the unreliable narrator" (45). Developing tactics of using negative space and noise, insinuation and intimation, key terms and multilingual interactions when it came to spoken word, Lemon, Profeta, and their collaborators arrived at the "freeing" conclusion "that language has the playful power to redirect and misdirect" (45). Similarly, narrative need not block access to "that elusive sense of presence" in the "electric now" of dance. Instead, it "is fruitfully impossible to sustain" immediacy outside of narrative (59). The now "eventually syncopates and spawns a narrative of how we entered or exited that particular state of grace." This inevitable "narrative understanding" is what "allows perception to make and retain an impact" (59). In both cases, language and text become crucial places in which the dramaturg has work to do: she brings a compositional sensitivity to how words might be used.

Part of why the dramaturg can do this effectively is that she is often a conductor of research alongside the choreographer and dancers. At least this was the case for Profeta in her work with Lemon. Research became "a prompt for conversation" and "an opportunity to locate the potential energy in what is fragmentary and seemingly strange" (70). Thinking of research as a springboard for making, Profeta contends that this approach "helps relieve us of that image of the dramaturg's research as a preproduction task to be checked off a list, or a completed collection of material to be delivered and taught." Rather, research becomes "a longer-term creative process to be shared, in

Ralph Lemon's *An All Day Event: The End*, Danspace Project, New York, 2012. Photograph: Ian Douglas

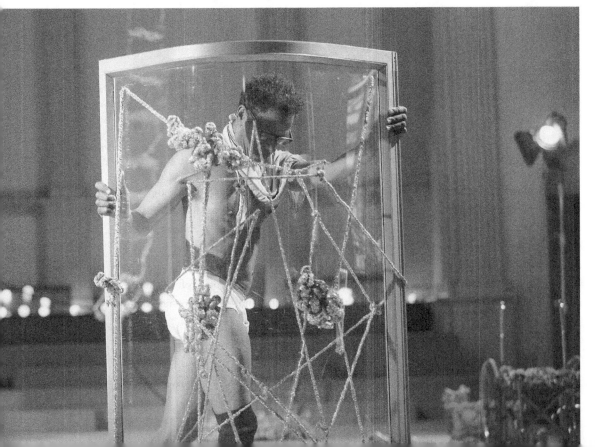

which the dramaturg is an active, perhaps even catalyzing participant, but not the sole responsible party" (70). This may almost threaten to make the dramaturg disposable, but Profeta instead posits that it saturates dance making with dramaturgical energies, fostering what she calls "active archives" (87) that can trigger the movement from collation to creation (71). For instance, when Ralph Lemon returned to his interest in the vernacular African American tradition of the buck dance for *Come Home Charley Patton*, Profeta brought in a 1987 documentary film by Mike Seeger, *Talking Feet: Solo Southern Dance: Flatfoot, Buck, and Tap*, for the group to view. They did so, but not to imitate the movement in it. Instead, Lemon urged his dancers to "find their own bucks." Profeta concludes that "the buck dance thus became the cast's tool for exploring received notions and cultural memories—those subjective provinces where past collides with present, history with fiction" (78). Thus, dramaturgical research helped to spark personal reworkings of the past rather than predigested wisdom. The dramaturg contributed by providing resources that shaped a guiding metaphor of the devised process. In this way, she too found her own buck within the larger collaborations.

If Profeta glimpses great opportunities for dramaturgical contributions when it comes to language and research, she is more hesitant about the dramaturg's traditional role as first audience member or "outside eye." Instead, Profeta is more interested in what André Lepecki calls the "invisible ghosts" of the audience that start to intrude on the creative process. She adds to this notion the idea of a "mutual haunting" in "the moment of spectatorship" when "the art-makers also become ghosts to the audience" (99). These specters across the lines of spectatorship can be vexing to deal with, particularly in terms of who gets to speak for whom: can Profeta speak for particular audiences authentically, or is her own identity a limiting factor? Ultimately, however, the idea of mutual haunting offers Profeta a sense of emancipation: the dramaturg herself can dance across the proscenium, free to contribute multiple perspectives from within or outside the performance. Sometimes her work involves helping the dance makers achieve an internal rigor and consistency that enables enriched receptions by an audience; sometimes it means advocating for tactics that encourage the uneasy experience of what Susan Manning calls "cross viewing,"[3] or the heightening of awareness by audience members of the differences of identity among them in viewing a work (particularly around issues of race) (117); sometimes her responses create some new direction in the process unanticipated by all, most of all herself. In the end, the dramaturg does not seek to represent the audience or the creators as much as to mediate between them, adding sparks to the mix, energizing the encounter between the two.

If Profeta resists the placement of the dramaturg in the role of surrogate for the audience, she cultivates the intersection of dramaturgical expertise with questions of movement that are at the heart of dance making. These might seem, at first, to be solely the precinct of the choreographer, but Profeta contends that a dramaturg can use her literacy in interpreting movement vocabularies through systems such as Laban analysis to "apprehend a richness of the 'how'" of movement. This "holds potential for even more" realization of "richness across the body or bodies in motion . . . or utter stillness." Analyzing movement with a perceptive literacy allows the dramaturg "to reflect . . . observation back in dialogue with the choreographer" so that a dance can achieve the precision and intensity required to deliver information and feeling most effectively (158). At the same time, the dramaturg can lead the way in the ongoing effort to discover fresh and innovative movement by purposefully abandoning her knowledge. When helping Lemon and his cast develop the wild Wall/Hole section of *How Can You . . . ?* Profeta points out that she "had to surrender my previously established competencies" as a dramaturg. This "reiterated . . . that the most urgent aspect of the dramaturg's job—her own source of motion—is to continually deskill and reskill her own faculties of perception, and to avoid carrying forward the competencies gained by a previous project, or even a previous moment, as a prescriptive blueprint for the next" (166).

In her final chapter, Profeta turns to the intercultural aspects of dance as an embodied cultural form. Because Lemon became interested in altering his own choreographic habits through extended encounters with dancers from other places, contexts, and people, his work grew deeply intercultural. This led Profeta to grapple with the difficult ethics of these collaborations and exchanges. She most fascinatingly relates Lemon's daring interest in having a farmer-musician from the Yunnan Province in rural China, Mr. Li, sing and play the *sanxian*, a plucked string instrument, in blackface. Since it sounded to the choreographer as if Mr. Li were making the sounds of "an old black man in the South" playing the banjo, Lemon wanted to "make blatant not just the comparison he was hearing but also how wrong it was—highlighting and making a point of the artificiality of the imposition" (197). But try as they might, Lemon and Profeta and various translators could never confirm that Mr. Li fully understood the gesture. Therefore, this left open troubling questions about intercultural consent. Ambiguous as Lemon's intercultural efforts were, they nonetheless were examples of what Patrice Pavis deems the value of risky "inter-corporeal work" (204).[4] As Profeta explains:

> I can verify that the political and historical implications of intercorporeal exchange were often felt in *Geography* and *Tree*'s rehearsal rooms. Frequently work on a tricky flight of dancing would spawn yet one more involved cast discussion about the dancers' reasons for dancing, the tensions between individual and group, the notion of "freedom," the residues of colonialism, or the connections between dance and spirituality. These topics bubbled up easily from just below the surface of the daily work, because they were so often implicit in the reasons for which one moved this way instead of that. As dramaturg, I felt that it was my job to acknowledge the power of effective intercorporeal exchange, recognize when we were in the midst

of that sort of work, figure out how to support that mode and keep us in the midst of it as long as possible, and document the impassioned dialogues, awkward tensions, and periodic epiphanies that extended from the time we spent there. (204–5)

Even Mr. Li found a way across the boundaries of cultural difference, surprising everyone one day during the making of *Tree* by suddenly starting to sing along with an old blues song by the famous Delta slide guitarist and singer Robert Johnson. "The potential of this surprise rang out crystal clear," Profeta remembers. "There was no contest; all agreed: this would be the final moment of the piece, hauntingly conveying both understanding and misunderstanding across a cultural gulf" (209).

From engagements with language and text to research to audience to movement to interculturalism, the relational work of dance dramaturgy becomes, for Profeta, something messy, impure, and often problematic—and yet, in its way, dance dramaturgy marks for her a pure gold standard of theatrical experience. It achieves both creative accomplishment and critical abstraction; it becomes a means of contributing to concrete artistic works that also crystallize larger stakes about identity, soci-

The Geography Trilogy, Part 3: Come Home Charley Patton, 2005. Photo: Dan Merlo

ety, and being alive in the contemporary world. Dance dramaturgy even offers a quiet kind of resistance to the atomization of knowledge through specialization. "In a culture full of specialists," Profeta argues, "dramaturgy offers one of the last refuges for the obstinate generalist" (xii). In a world of routinization, it sets its sights on the work of wide-ranging exploration. As Profeta puts it, dramaturgy "offers a field of activity for those who would like nothing more than to engage, repeatedly, in what the education field has dubbed 'project-based learning'—to kindle a fascination with a set of questions, around the formation of an impending event, and then stoke that fascination by approaching it from as many different angles, as many different knowledge bases, as are possibly relevant (and a few that aren't, for good measure)" (xii). While this oddly mirrors, indeed exemplifies, a broader transition to the economic insecurities of a precarious "creative class," Profeta is less focused on an approach that links dance to structural issues of labor than the close-up experiences of identity politics as they run through choreographic creation and movement performance.

For Profeta, dance dramaturgy provides a means of direct encounters with themes that fascinate, as well as with people driven to investigate these fascinations with body and soul. In writing about her dramaturgical experiences, she provides an illuminating study of Ralph Lemon's powerful work. So, too, she is among the first to probe the theoretical issues of dramaturgy as an emergent practice within dance making. "A renewable curiosity is the dramaturg's main stock-in-trade," Profeta proposes (xii), and she herself has written a book that, as it pivots between a specific collaboration and the larger developing field of dance dramaturgy, repeatedly remakes motion into something to think about.

Notes

1. Jenn Joy, *The Choreographic* (Cambridge, MA: MIT Press, 2014), 1.
2. See, for example, Pil Hansen and Darcey Callison, eds., *Dance Dramaturgy: Modes of Agency, Awareness, and Engagement* (New York: Springer, 2015).
3. Susan Manning, *Modern Dance, Negro Dance: Race in Motion* (Minneapolis: University of Minnesota Press, 2004), 117.
4. Patrice Pavis, "Introduction: Towards a Theory of Interculturalism in the Theatre?," in *The Intercultural Performance Reader*, ed. Patrice Pavis (London: Routledge, 1996), 1–21.

Theater 47:1   DOI 10.1215/01610775-3710580

JONATHAN KALB

THE ANTIPROFESSIONAL PREJUDICE

Directing Scenes and Senses: The Thinking of Regie
by Peter M. Boenisch
Manchester: Manchester University Press, 2015

I dream sometimes of all German directors of plays with perhaps one exception united in one with
his back to the wall and me shooting a bullet into his balls every five minutes till he loses his taste for
improving authors.
—Samuel Beckett, letter to Alan Schneider, January 4, 1960

The clash of civilizations over what theater directing is supposed to be has been rag-
ing for more than half a century. Beckett's famous implacability regarding play-
wrights' authority reflects one polar extreme that has become a cultural cliché. The
expressionist-era Austrian actor Fritz Kortner's quip "Fidelity to texts is stupidity!"
might be a flag for the other pole. The battle is really between warring cultural cari-
catures: Anglophone theater as a puritanical haven of textual fundamentalism versus
German theater—trendsetter for continental Europe—as a bedlam of arbitrariness and
degraded classics. Another common spin is Anglophone theater as a desert of ossified
tradition and commercial corruption versus German theater as a circus of subsidized
egomania and rationalized nonsense. Everyone with intimate experience of both cul-

Thomas Ostermeier's
Richard III,
Schaubühne am
Lehniner Platz,
Berlin, 2015.
Photo: Arno Declair,
courtesy of Schaubühne
am Lehniner Platz

tures knows how stale and inadequate these
clichés are, yet they persist, perpetually reac-
tivated by both journalists and academics.

A smart, well-informed book that man-
ages to bridge this divide, clearly explaining the opposing values with an aim toward
reducing misunderstandings and fostering
mutual sympathy and curiosity, would be an
extraordinary boon. And Peter Boenisch, a
German who moved to the United Kingdom
to teach more than ten years ago, would seem
ideally situated to provide it. Alas, *Directing
Scenes and Senses* is not the needed book. It
is a densely theoretical, gratuitously abstruse

philosophical discussion that makes sweeping claims about contemporary theater while closely considering only a very narrow slice of it (about eighteen German, Dutch, and Flemish productions seen between 2004 and 2014). Boenisch argues that continental *Regie* is an independent art distinct from the practical task of staging plays—a view many others have expressed (including Hans-Thies Lehmann, Erika Fischer-Lichte, and Marvin Carlson), which Boenisch seeks to affirm with strained historical associations to distant figures like Schiller and Hegel and an obfuscating torrent of adulatory references to contemporary theorists.

The first half of the book lays out his analytical case in a series of tortuous pseudo-arguments, focusing on arcane disputations over philosophical categories unleavened by clarifying historical evidence and providing a deeply deficient précis of the eighteenth- and nineteenth-century roots of directing in general that omits almost all non-Germans. Brits who are crucial to the larger genesis story, for instance, such as David Garrick, William Poel, and Harley Granville-Barker, are never mentioned. The artists who are named are certainly germane (e.g., Schiller, Goethe, Conrad Ekhof, August Wilhelm Iffland, Heinrich Laube), but no development is traced between them and the present. The prose is appalling, and reading Boenisch means trudging through clotted and rambling Engleutsch sentences like this on practically every page:

> While for [Franz von Akáts], as he makes clear from the outset, the practice of *mise en scène* did not imply an "original creation [*eigene Schöpfung*]", he also reminds us of the fact that what we today, from a Continental perspective, understand as a primarily, if not solely artistic practice emerged to no negligible extent from an economic context—not at all unlike the English theatre producer, who, even in present-day direction, remains caught between "artistry and organization," where the latter may even be "the crucial and defining activity of direction" (21).

The book's second half applies this analytical wisdom, such as it is, to seven directors and one company—Jürgen Gosch, Michael Thalheimer, tg STAN, Andreas Kriegenburg, Ivo van Hove, Guy Cassiers, Frank Castorf, and Thomas Ostermeier—some of whose work has been seen in the United States. This section is helpfully informative about plainly valuable productions one has not seen; it contains tolerably clear descriptions and a few interesting artists' statements translated for the first time. Unfortunately, Boenisch presents the case studies almost entirely sui generis, isolated from theatrical activity beyond the central European domain of *Regie* he cherishes. No comparable productions by others of the classical plays in question are ever considered, even though some were originally written in English. In this way, too, he squanders a chance to build bridges and influence the Anglophone conversation.

Boenisch is unhappy about directing's ambiguous terminology. He wishes the terms *direction*, *mise-en-scène*, and *Regie* were not used interchangeably. *Direction* should be used only for "the *practical* aspect of putting a playtext on stage and mounting a production . . . the craft and labour of making theatre" (189). *Mise-en-scène* should be "an *analytic* concept which expresses the dynamic process of emitting and releasing the playtext on stage" (190). *Regie*, by contrast, should be a purely "*aesthetic* concept" referring to a posture of "dissensus" toward practical and economic theatrical contingencies and a liberatory ideal of adventurous, communal interpretation and risky discovery. Note how the English term rides in labor-class steerage while the German soars aristocratically in free aesthetic contemplation.

It irks Boenisch that practitioners of *Regie* are often seen as headstrong egomaniacs parading their interpretive idiosyncrasies before an indulgent and star-struck public. A worthy *Regisseur*, for him, is not merely an interpreter of canonical texts containing settled intentions, historical contexts, and meanings. He (almost never she—the profession is overwhelmingly male) is a "medium" (25), a sensitive collaborative artist engaged in playful "speculative thinking" (42) and dedicated to fostering such thinking in others. The utopian vision of Jacques Rancière's 2009 book *The Emancipated Spectator* supplies Boenisch's central thesis. *Regie* is used as a relational term in Rancière's slow-cooking radical spirit—an anti-authoritarian practice that emancipates spectators by refusing to treat them as "ignoramuses" who must absorb the superior knowledge of great artists. The

Ivo Van Hove and Toneelgroep Amsterdam's *Roman Tragedies*, the Holland Festival, Amsterdam, 2007. Photo: Jan Versweyveld

Regisseur (Boenisch implies without naming the figure) is ideally like Rancière's "ignorant schoolmaster" who teaches others what he himself doesn't know, validating "equality of intelligence" and inviting all manner of unpredictable responses that pave the way for a new "politics of the sensible." Quoting Rancière, Boenisch says: "*Regie* creates and celebrates the shared communities of 'active interpreters, who develop their own translations in order to appropriate the "story" and make it their own'" (192).

Boenisch's other guiding light is Slavoj Žižek, whose eccentric and extraordinarily complex, thousand-page book *Less than Nothing: Hegel and the Shadow of Dialectical Materialism* (2012) reads Hegel through Lacan while analyzing all of German philosophical idealism (Kant, Fichte, Schelling) as well as Buddhism, Christianity, Marxism, Plato, Heidegger, Kafka, sexuality, quantum physics, and innumerable other subjects. Žižek proposes a radical view of dialectical materialism that (to simplify grossly) embraces certain species of error in the name of "engaged subjectivity": "What

appears to us as our inability to know the thing indicates a crack in the thing itself, so that our very failure to reach the full truth is the indicator of truth," writes Žižek in a passage not cited in Boenisch (Žižek, 17). One concrete example of Žižek's is used as an illustration: "The cinema version of Doctorow's *Billy Bathgate* is basically a failure, but an interesting one: a failure which nonetheless evokes in the viewer the specter of a much better novel" (Žižek, 617). For Boenisch, this example offers "a principal argument against the misinformed perception of the director as authoritarian *auteur* who allegedly (ab)uses the playwright's work according to his individual whim" (46). Abuse is inconceivable and irrelevant where a "work" amounts to "the inscription of the subject itself (its gaze or desire) into the object" (Žižek, 617). Boenisch furthermore believes that Schiller supported this idea in his well-known essay "On the Use of the Chorus in Tragedy"; his reflections on the mediating role of the chorus supposedly anticipated the radical "freedom" of *Regie*.

Here's the wrinkle. It's one thing to play the time-honored academic game of cherry-picking hoary quotations and stringing them together with poststructuralist platitudes to make every historical figure, even those two hundred years dead, seem like the same Foucauldian death-of-the-author theorist. All theorymongers do that. It's quite another to use a complex, radically revisionist theory of dialectical materialism to justify a view of *Regietheater* that ignores the material conditions in which the art is made. That's more like demagoguery. His passing reference to Akáts aside, Boenisch is silent on the economic and institutional circumstances that support the theater he so admires: nary a word from him on the enormous public subsidies in Germany (and elsewhere) that finance full-time ensemble repertory companies that can devote themselves to his sort of open and playful explorations in six-month rehearsal-workshops. He sneers at "pragmatic Anglo-American theatre production" (89) and "the day-to-day business of getting the curtain up" (91), disdaining "the imperative of 'doing the play(text)' and 'producing a show'" (191), as well as "U.S. ideology [that] . . . privileges, above all, the individual" (37). Yet he is blind to the privileged circumstances of central European *Regie* and the ideology that underlies it.

The subsidized state and city theaters of Europe are enviable institutions. They bring much light to the theater and the world, sometimes in the way Boenisch prizes, by fostering adventurous forms of communal interpretation and translation. (So do many British and American directors and theaters, even occasionally commercial ones.) Yet the continental Stadts- and Staatstheater also have serious downsides; for example, ignoring new work in favor of classics, protecting complacency, and fueling celebrity worship of *Regisseure*. Some *Regisseure* may indeed aspire to the condition of "ignorant schoolmasters," but the ones idolized as stars by European public relations machines often fall into mannerism, self-indulgence, and narcissism. Boenisch says nothing about this. He avoids questions of evaluation entirely, evidently regarding all *Regietheater* as equal in quality. In a footnote he mentions that "many regular performers and dramaturgs left the Volksbühne" in the mid-2000s due to Frank Castorf's behavior as a director but then says no more about it. What makes a Castorf production bad, from his colleagues' viewpoint? Or from the public's? Or from a sympathetic critic's? It would be interesting to know what Boenisch thinks.

I've seen work by most of the directors he uses as main examples. Three I know very well, and I can confidently assert that their productions range hugely in quality and ambition. Ivo van Hove, for instance, whose work I've seen a dozen times, has thrilled me (*More Stately Mansions*, *Antigone*), bored me (*The Misanthrope*, *The Crucible*), and evoked countless other reactions including grudging respect (*Roman Tragedies*, *The Little Foxes*). It's evasive and disingenuous to attribute such differences solely to the dice roll of subjective response. Van Hove's *Misanthrope*, I would insist, was shallow in its own right. I couldn't care less whether it respected or heeded Molière. My point isn't about textual fidelity but, rather, quality of reading—reading understood in a broad sense to include the director and company's observations of life and connections to the current world, which always set the bar for a production's present-tense power. *The Misanthrope*'s principal artistic gambit—enacting the play's climactic debate about aristocratic hypocrisy as a prolonged food fight—was simply monotonous and obvious. (Get it? The refined people are really vulgar!)

Another example: van Hove's five-and-a-half-hour *Roman Tragedies*, lavishly praised by Boenisch for the "parallax perspective" created when audiences were invited onstage to commune around an open bar and café seats, with the Shakespeare scenes continuing amid multiple distractions, including large-screen televisions showing current war news and "live interviews" with Shakespeare's fictional political leaders. This was indeed an amusingly excessive way of reminding the audience that it shared responsibility for violence like that dramatized in the play, but it also grew tedious and cumbersome over time, and the Shakespeare action wasn't gripping or moving enough to sustain deep involvement on its own. In other words, *Regie* may sometimes rise to Boenisch's lofty emancipatory ideal, but it's just as often an alibi for broad-brushing, overgeneralizing, and laziness (the familiar cheat of cutting what one can't solve from a source text so that it appears to be a simpler problem).

There is an insidious antiprofessional prejudice behind any book-length effort to bypass theater's messy practical circumstances and consider it purely via immaculate abstract ideals. The devil is always in the professional details of a utopian vision. To suggest, as Boenisch does, that "the imperative of 'doing the play(text)'" is the categorical opposite of "an attitude of playfulness that fosters thinking and imagining" (191) is not only to imply that all who question *Regie* are literalists, dupes of the spectacle society, and slaves of consumerism. It's also to demonstrate shocking insensitivity to playtexts and ignorance of theater beyond the hermetic bubble of *Regietheater*.

Cultivated Americans and Brits are perfectly able to appreciate the achievements of *Regisseure* like van Hove, Castorf, Ostermeier, and Thalheimer. Yet Boenisch seems unable to see the slightest value in the thrilling close-textual explorations of, say, Michael Boyd, Gregory Doran, or Declan Donnellan's Shakespeare projects. So averse is Boenisch to professional context that he ignores obvious points that could support his thesis, such as the intense personal rivalries that exist among *Regisseure*, which sometimes turn their productions into fascinating intertextual conversations and prompt roughly simultaneous dueling productions of the same play (e.g., Ostermeier's and Thalheimer's versions of Wedekind's *Lulu* in 2004). So indifferent is Boenisch to factual background that he misses basic information about his examples. For instance, that *Scenes from a Marriage* was first adapted for the stage by Ingmar Bergman himself (at a *German* theater!) and not by van Hove. In these ways, he falsifies the extent to which his revered *Regisseure* actually do care about such matters as literary context, authorial intention, and historical precedent.

George Steiner once wrote (speaking of criticism) that "to read well is to take great risks," because it requires openness, imagination, and humility as well as intelligence, experience, and sensitivity to language.[1] This sort of sage risk taking is obviously endangered in our increasingly visual and digital age, and one reason why is the steady disappearance of criticism of the sort Steiner advocated. Like all artists, directors need to know that intelligent, informed, invested, and independent observers are following what they do closely and can make their voices heard in a public conversation. Failing that, even the best artists will succumb to the lures of celebrity and commerce and grow flabby, lazy, and glib. In light of all this, there is nothing to be gained from yet another baffling theoretical harangue on *Regie* that reinforces partisan divisions. In place of esoteric hermeneutics, we need an intelligibly demanding erotics of theater criticism.

NOTE

1. George Steiner. 1998. *Language and Silence: Essays on Language, Literature, and the Inhuman.* New Haven: Yale University Press, 10. The source essay, "Humane Literacy," is from 1963.

Theater 47:1   DOI 10.1215/01610775-3710592
© 2017 by Jonathan Kalb

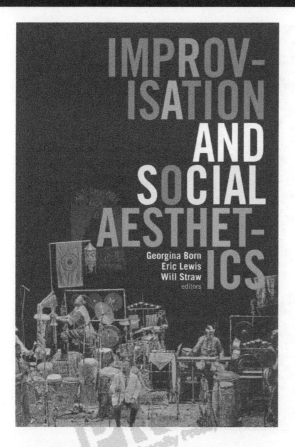

Illegible Will

Coercive Spectacles of Labor in South Africa
and the Diaspora

HERSHINI BHANA YOUNG

7 illustrations, paper, $28.95

"Illegible Will is, in short, a masterpiece. While it is common to find a book able to shed new light on well-worn material, or that engages with a completely new archive, it is exceedingly rare to find a book that does both. This is such a book.... A highly imaginative, poetic, and creative approach to the archive, Illegible Will is of tremendous value for those in performance studies, black studies, literature, queer studies, and dance studies." — ***Uri McMillan***

DUKE UNIVERSITY PRESS

Printed and bound by CPI Group (UK) Ltd, Croydon, CR0 4YY

13/04/2025

14656486-0004